A HISTORY OF
THE
COMSTOCK SILVER LODE & MINES

NEVADA AND THE GREAT BASIN REGION;

LAKE TAHOE AND THE HIGH SIERRAS.

THE MOUNTAINS, VALLEYS, LAKES, RIVERS, HOT SPRINGS, DESERTS, AND OTHER WONDERS OF THE "EASTERN SLOPE" OF THE SIERRAS.

THE
MINERAL AND AGRICULTURAL RESOURCES
OF
"SILVERLAND."

TOWNS, SETTLEMENTS, MINING AND REDUCTION WORKS, RAILWAYS, LUMBER FLUMES, PINE FORESTS, SYSTEMS OF WATER SUPPLY, GREAT SHAFTS AND TUNNELS, AND THE MANY IMPROVEMENTS AND INDUSTRIES OF NEVADA.

BY DAN DE QUILLE,
author of

"The Big Bonanza,"
The Wealth and Wonders of Washoe.
The Arid Zone and Irrigation, Etc.

PUBLISHED BY F. BOEGLE,
BOOKSELLER & STATIONER,
VIRGINIA, NEVADA.

Entered According to Act of Congress, in the Year 1889, by

F. BOEGLE,

In the Office of the Librarian of Congress, at Washington.

NEW YORK AND SAN FRANCISCO,
PACIFIC PRESS PUBLISHING COMPANY,
OAKLAND, CAL.,
PRINTERS, STATIONERS, AND BINDERS.

In the interest of creating a more extensive selection of rare historical book reprints, we have chosen to reproduce this title even though it may possibly have occasional imperfections such as missing and blurred pages, missing text, poor pictures, markings, dark backgrounds and other reproduction issues beyond our control. Because this work is culturally important, we have made it available as a part of our commitment to protecting, preserving and promoting the world's literature. Thank you for your understanding.

INTRODUCTORY.

The central idea in the preparation of this little book has been to give, as concisely as possible, such information in regard to the silver mines of the Comstock as the visiting tourist is likely to require. In doing this it was thought best to begin by briefly introducing the whole State of Nevada. When shown a portion of a thing we generally have some curiosity in regard to the appearance of the whole. Though much more space has been given to the mines, mining works, towns, and industries of the Comstock Lode than to anything else, yet it has been found necessary to the plan of the work to include much of surrounding regions, both in Nevada and California. However, we have endeavored to keep on the "Eastern slope" of the Sierras—have poached very little on the California side. The Sierra Nevada Mountains are a towering, rocky range, which constitutes a natural dividing line between the regions of country on either side. All on the east side of the Sierras partakes more of the general character of Nevada

INTRODUCTION.

than of California—is characteristic of the Great Basin region. Although Owens River, Independence and Owens Valleys, Owens Lake and Mono Lake, are within the boundaries of California, yet they are essentially parts of that region the whole of which is known as the Great Basin.

In speaking of the Comstock Lode, after giving an account of its discovery and something of its early history, it has been necessary in noting the progress of our towns and the improvements made in mining and milling operations and methods to go up into the Sierras to trace our water supply to its sources. It is also from the great pine forests of the Sierras that we derive our supply of lumber and timbers, and the Sierras are our natural sanitarium—it is to the lakes, valleys, and wilds of the "High Sierras" that our summer pleasure trips are made. For this reason mention has been made of lakes, valleys, mountains, and creeks not strictly our own—though a large slice of Lake Tahoe lies within our boundaries.

In mentioning rivers, lakes, and railroads it has also been thought best to say something of all in the State. In the case of the railrords it became necessary to speak briefly of the towns they connect and pass through, with a passing glance at the country traversed.

INTRODUCTION.

Although the Comstock Lode, and mining and milling in Western Nevada, are the principal subjects of this book, yet it is not wholly a book on Nevada. "No pent-up Utica" has for a moment been permitted to "contract our powers." We have been guided more by the natural than the political divisions of the country, therefore our little book takes in the western edge of the Great Basin, climbing up to the top of the Sierras, and peeping over in a few places.

viii CONTENTS.

VIEWS FROM THE CITY AND VICINITY................. 58
THE VIEW FROM THE SUMMIT OF MOUNT DAVIDSON,... 59
THE VIRGINIA AND TRUCKEE RAILROAD.............. 59
THE DAYS OF BULL TEAMS........................... 61
THE COMSTOCK SYSTEM OF WATER SUPPLY............ 63
THE VIRGINIA CITY AND GOLD HILL WATER WORKS ... 63
THE BIG WATER PIPES............................... 65
THE SUTRO TUNNEL.................................. 68
THE REDUCTION WORKS OF EARLY DAYS............... 70
THE FIRST SILVER MILL............................. 70
THE MANY MILLS OF THE EARLY DAYS................ 72
REDUCTION WORKS OF THE PRESENT DAY.............. 74
DESCRIPTION OF THE PROCESS OF WORKING COMSTOCK
    SILVER ORES...................................... 74
THE TWO CALIFORNIA MILLS,........................ 80
THE RIVER AND CANYON MILLS 81
THE COMSTOCK LODE............................. 82
    Hoisting Works, Shafts and Mining, Past and Present... 82
    The Three Lines of Hoisting Works.................... 84
THE COMBINATION SHAFT 86
    The Deepest Workings on the Lode.................. 88
    A Return to the Second Line of Works 89
    The Old First Bonanzas............................. 91
    The New Departure................................. 92
    Present Yield of the Comstock Mines.................. 93
    Vicissitudes of Fortune in Mining 96
TOWNS OF WESTERN NEVADA.................... 98
    Virginia City.. 96
    Gold Hill 97
    Silver City... 101
    Dayton.. 102
    Sutro 104
    Carson City.. 105
    Empire City.. 109

CONTENTS.

Genoa..110
Reno...111
OTHER TOWNS IN WASHOE COUNTY....................113
   Washoe City...113
   Ophir...114
   Franktown...114
LAKE TAHOE AND SURROUNDINGS...........................115
   Emerald Bay...121
   Fallen Leaf Lake....................................123
   Silver Lake...123
   Cornelian Bay.......................................123
   Agate Bay...123
   Crystal Bay...123
   Shakespeare Rock....................................123
   Cave Rock...124
   Glenbrook...124
   Cascade Mountain....................................124
   Rubicon Springs.....................................124
ROUTES TO LAKE TAHOE..................................125
THE ROUTE FROM TRUCKEE................................125
DISTANCES FROM TAHOE CITY TO POINTS ON THE LAKE.126
THE ROUTE FROM RENO...................................127
THE TOWN OF TRUCKEE...................................128
DONNER LAKE...129
THE DONNER DISASTER...................................130
SURROUNDING POINTS OF INTEREST........................131
INDEPENDENCE LAKE AND SURROUNDINGS....................132
WEBBER LAKE WONDERS..................................133
PYRAMID LAKE..134
WINNEMUCCA LAKE......................................136
WASHOE LAKE..138
THERMAL AND MEDICINAL SPRINGS........................138
   Steamboat Springs...................................139
   Shaw's Springs......................................141

CONTENTS.

State Prison Warm Springs..........................141
Walley's Springs..................................142
Other Nevada Springs..............................143
RAILROADS IN NEVADA...............................144
THE CENTRAL PACIFIC...............................145
VIRGINIA AND TRUCKEE DISTANCES....................146
THE CARSON AND COLORADO...........................146
    Wabuska......................................147
    Hawthorne....................................148
    Luning.......................................148
    Bellville....................................148
    Candelaria...................................148
    Benton.......................................149
    Bishop Creek.................................149
    Independence.................................149
    Keeler.......................................150
OWENS LAKE..150
MONO LAKE...151
EUREKA AND PALISADE RAILROAD......................151
    Town of Palisade.............................151
    Eureka.......................................151
NEVADA CENTRAL RAILROAD...........................152
    Town of Battle Mountain......................152
    Austin.......................................153
NEVADA AND CALIFORNIA RAILROAD....................154
PROPOSED RAILROADS................................154
SALT LAKE AND LOS ANGELES.........................155
NEVADA, CENTRAL, AND IDAHO........................155

The State of Nevada.

Boundaries and Area.

NEVADA is formed of the region of country formerly known as Western Utah. The whole of Utah, prior to its acquisition by the United States, was a portion of the Mexican Department of Alta California. All this vast region was acquired from Mexico under the treaty of Guadalupe Hidalgo, which was consummated in 1848, and which treaty also gave to the United States, California, Arizona, New Mexico, and a part of Colorado. Nevada was constituted a Territory in March, 1861, and was admitted into the Union as a State in October, 1864. The State extends from the 35th to the 42d degree of north latitude, and from the 114th to the 120th degree west longitude from Greenwich. The State in its greatest dimensions is 420 miles long by 360 miles wide. Nevada is bounded on the north by Idaho and Oregon, east by Utah and Arizona, and south and west by California. Previous to its acquisition by the United States, the region now constituting the State of Nevada was wholly occupied by tribes of wild Indians. The country was then known only to a few white men, trappers and Indian traders, whose business at certain seasons led them into what was then almost a *terra incognito*, and which was marked upon the maps of that day as the "Great American Desert," or the "Unexplored Region."

The area of the State is, by the most reliable estimate, 112,190 square miles, or 71,801,819 acres. This includes what is known as the "Colorado Basin," in Lincoln County, on the southern boundary of the State, and which embraces an area of about 12,000 square miles lying north of the Colorado River. This basin region was taken from Arizona and given to Nevada by an Act of Congress in 1866. Assuming the water surface of the numerous lakes in Nevada to cover an area of 1,690 square miles, or 1,081,-819 acres, there remain 110,500 square miles, or 70,-720,000 acres as the land area of the State. The vastness of this region is not at once grasped by the mind of the reader. It may be more readily realized by comparison with some of the well-known Eastern States. The area of Nevada is 2,578 square miles greater than the combined areas of Maine, New Hampshire, Vermont, Connecticut, Massachusetts, Maryland, Delaware, West Virginia, New Jersey, and Rhode Island. Indeed, after giving to each of the States named its full measure of acres, there would be left enough land to make two additional Rhode Islands. In all this great territory, however, there are only about 62,000 souls. Belgium, with an area of 11,373 square miles, has a population of 5,253,821, or about 462 persons to the square mile, and there the rural population is to that of the towns as three to one. Were Nevada as densely peopled as Belgium it would contain 51,749,780 souls, a number almost equal to the present population of the whole United States. It will therefore be seen that before becoming as thickly settled as is Belgium, Nevada still has room for 51,687,780 persons within her boundaries.

The Sierra Nevada Mountains from the western boundary of Nevada for a distance of over 300 miles, constitute a stupendous snow-capped granite wall between the State and California. The mean height of this part of the Sierra Nevada Range is about 7,000 feet. This towering range has a marked effect on the climate of Nevada. But for its intervention the climate of the whole State would be much the same as that of California.

The Physical Aspect of Nevada.

Though the western edge laps up onto the Sierra Nevada Range, the greater part of the State of Nevada lies to the eastward and is embraced in that Great Basin region which extends to the western base of the Rocky Mountains. This interior region forms an immense plateau which has a mean elevation of four thousand feet above the level of the sea. In Nevada, however, the average altitude of the plateau may safely be set down at five thousand feet. The altitude of White Plains Station, west of the sink of the Humboldt, is 3,894 feet, and it is the lowest point on the overland railroad between the Sierra Nevada and the Rocky Mountains. Owing to this great elevation there is in all parts of Nevada an atmosphere pure, dry, and free from even the slightest malarial taint. It is such an atmosphere as in many other lands can only be found by going to the mountain tops. The average level of the State is higher than many of the noted mountain resorts in the Atlantic States. It is owing to this altitude that the nights in summer are always cool and pleasant, however warm the weather during the hours of daylight. The extremes of heat and cold are not great.

Running north and south through the elevated plateau which forms the general base or floor of the State are numerous parallel ranges of mountains. These interior ranges are quite regular in course and recurrence, and rise to a height of from one thousand to seven thousand feet above the general level of the country. Among these interior mountains are a few peaks that attain an elevation of from 9,000 to 12,000 feet above the level of the sea. Between these mountain ranges lie valleys ranging in width from one mile to thirty miles. As these valleys are hidden by the high, rocky ranges, and are not to be seen in a general survey of the country, even from an elevated position, the aspect of the country is sterile and austere, all being apparently a succession of barren, rocky hills.

The majority of the valleys lying between these rugged, parallel ranges are susceptible of cultivation, and many are wonderfully productive. The bench lands bordering the valleys are also exceedingly fertile and yield large crops wherever water for irrigation is led upon them. For all uses, those of the horticulturist as well as the agriculturist, these bench lands will yet be found the best in the State. The benches possess a warm and willing soil.

The interior mountains, rugged and timberless as they are, have their uses. From the summits of many of the ranges flow springs and small streams that afford a supply of water for the irrigation of the valley and bench lands below. They are also conservators of a supply of moisture. On the summits of the higher ranges snow falls in winter to a great depth, and from the melting of this in spring and summer is derived a considerable supply of water for use on the arable lands on either side. These reserves of snow are also of great benefit to the mountain pastures, causing grass to spring up along the courses of a thousand ravines and little valleys, or laps of land, on the slopes and tops of the hills. This water supply may be made infinitely more valuable than it is at present by the construction of suitable reservoirs at proper points in the large canyons for storing it up till needed in summer.

The construction of such reservoirs has already been commenced among the interior ranges, as well as in places along the main Sierra Nevada Range, and year by year more and still more such improvements will be made. Already Nevada holds a high place as an agricultural and stock-growing State, though for nearly the whole term of her existence mining for the precious metals has been the all-absorbing business of the majority of her people, and has been the business which has attracted the attention of nearly all the wealthy men of the country. The State annually produces immense quantities of hay, and the beef cattle of Nevada are the finest and fattest to be found on the Pacific Coast. A great part of the beef supply of California is obtained from Nevada. The horses of Nevada are also very fine and noted for their "staying" qualities, as they have much broader chests and larger lungs than the animals reared in valley regions near the level of the sea. The State is also beginning to make its mark in the business of wool-growing, not only on account of the quantity but also the quality produced. In price Nevada wool leads the wools of all the new regions of the West. Fine wheat and good grain of all kinds will everywhere be found in Nevada, and the apples, peaches, pears, plums, and all other kinds of fruit have a piquancy of flavor not to be found in that grown in the sweltering valleys of

California. The same may be said of all kinds of kitchen vegetables, strawberries, and other small fruits. In the way of potatoes the State produces such as have no superiors in any part of the world. This elevated region seems as much the natural home of the potato as were those high valleys in the Andes where it was first found growing wild, and where it is said the wild tuber is still to be seen.

The Rivers of Nevada.

Nevada has within her borders no large rivers. In the Middle and Western States, her so-called rivers would be rated as large brooks or creeks. In England and some other European countries her streams might pass for rivers. The largest river we have is but a rill in comparison with the rivers of the West and South. Our Nevada rivers, too, are peculiar in that they nearly all remain in the State. But one goes outside of our boundaries to wander away in search of the great ocean. Most of our streams stay at home. Rather than run away to be tossed about and lost in the sea, they go down into the ground or up into the air.

HUMBOLDT RIVER.

The Humboldt River rises in the northwestern corner of Utah, passes into the northeastern corner of Nevada, in Elko County, and thence through Eureka, Lander, and Humboldt Counties, to its terminus in its lake and sink, just across the line in Churchill County.

The total length of the river is nearly 350 miles, while its width is only about thirty or forty feet, and its average depth less than eighteen inches. The line of the Central Pacific Railroad follows the course of the stream a distance of about 320 miles, its channel forming a natural depression through the country which greatly facilitated the construction of the road. Down its course also lay the route followed by the emigrants who flocked across the "Plains" to California after the discovery of the gold mines. The water of the Humboldt is very bright and sweet toward the head, but near the "sink" the stream becomes rather sluggish and is somewhat tainted by the alkali absorbed in the lower part of its course. Owing to the increased use of water for the irrigation of bordering lands above, the quantity flowing into the lake each year grows smaller. The water carried out of the river by means of ditches to the valley ranches is dissipated by absorption and evaporation and never reaches the terminal lake. Thus it is seen as a result that the lake is gradually drying up. It will probably eventually become extinct, or survive as a mud marsh. In the spring, when the snow is melting about the head-waters of the river, Humboldt Lake has a length of about fifteen miles and a width of nine or ten miles. In summer and toward fall it becomes much smaller. At the south end of this lake is an outlet into a sink, or shallow lake, twenty-five or thirty miles long by about fifteen wide. This sink at times of high water connects with a similar sink formed by the overflow from Carson Lake, the terminal basin of the Carson River. In these sinks are found in the alkaline waters myriads of small fish. These attract immense flocks of pelicans, gulls, cranes, and other fish-eating water fowl. At certain seasons the lakes, sinks, and surrounding tule marshes are filled with ducks and geese. Large flocks of swan are also often seen out in the middle of the lakes. There is much fine agricultural and grazing land along down the Humboldt River, and about the lake and sink.

TRUCKEE RIVER.

Truckée River is one of the most beautiful of the streams of Nevada. It takes its rise in California and its head is an outlet from Lake Tahoe. This outlet is on the northwest side of the lake and is about fifty feet in width. It has an average depth of five feet and a velocity of six feet a second, which gives a flow of about 123,120,000 cubic feet in twenty-four hours. The head of the river is in Placer County, California, it runs nearly north into Nevada County, in the same State, to the town of Truckee, when it turns and flows northeast till it enters the State of Nevada at Verdi, in Washoe County. Its course from Verdi to Reno, the county seat of Washoe County, is nearly east, thence it is northeast to the town of Wadsworth, on the Central Pacific, when it suddenly turns to the north, and, after a course of about twenty-five miles, enters Pyramid Lake.

From the outlet of Lake Tahoe to Pyramid Lake the distance is about 100 miles.

After leaving Tahoe the Truckee receives the waters of many mountain streams. Below Verdi it passes through many beautiful and fertile valleys and meadows. Pyramid Lake has an elevation of 4,000 feet above the level of the sea; Lake Tahoe is 6,247 feet above sea-level, therefore between the two points the river has a fall of 2,247 feet, an average of a little over twenty-two feet to the mile. Along the river from end to end there is almost unlimited water power, there being a great volume of water, during several months, and an abundance of fall. This water-power is utilized at Reno to some extent, but what has been done there is merely a commencement toward what should be done. Large areas of land are irrigated by ditches leading out of the Truckee at several points. The stream is filled with beautiful trout of two or three species, and also contains other smaller fishes of several kinds. A kind sometimes seen in its waters at the spawning seasons is a large fish of the sucker tribe, which runs up from Pyramid Lake, and is called "koo-ee-wa" by the Piutes. It is half head, and in every respect is a very ugly fish. It is said that the "koo-ee-wa" is found nowhere else in the world. It is a palatable and wholesome fish, but its appearance is against it. The Piutes spear and cure (by drying in the sun) great quantities of this fish. Several kinds of Eastern fish have been planted in the waters of the Truckee and have been found to flourish. Fish ladders have been placed at all the dams in the rivers to permit of the trout and other fish ascending toward the head-waters to spawn in the various tributary creeks.

The Truckee River is named after "Captain Truckee," a Piute chief who in the early days guided a party of emigrants from the Humboldt to the beautiful stream and thence through Henness Pass across the Sierras to California. Captain Truckee also acted as a guide for Colonel Fremont when he passed through the country in 1846. He died in the Como Mountains in 1860, from the bite of some poisonous insect, and was there buried by members of his tribe, and whites, with much sorrow. A description of Pyramid Lake will be given further along, as it deserves a separate notice, being the largest lake wholly owned by Nevada, and almost as large as the Great Salt Lake, in Utah, which is seventy miles in length by about thirty in width.

CARSON RIVER.

The Carson River rises in the Sierras and has several tributaries across the line in California, in Alpine County. The river is about 220 miles in length and ends in Carson Lake. It enters Nevada in Douglas County. It has two branches, known as the East Fork and the West Fork. These unite near the town of Genoa, the county seat of Douglas County. The river then plows through the center of Douglas County into Ormsby, passing near Carson City, the capital of the State, thence into Lyon County, and finally finds its terminal "sink" in Carson Lake, in Churchill County. This lake has an outlet several miles in length into a second lake, or sink, which at times of great freshets is united with the lower sink of the Humboldt, as has already been mentioned. Carson Lake is circular in form and is about twelve miles long and eight or nine in width. It has a depth of forty or fifty feet, and its waters are quite sweet. The lower sink is about twenty miles long and from four to eight miles wide. Its waters, particularly toward the north end, where it is very shallow, are strongly alkaline. These lakes are at times resorted to by great flocks of all kinds of water fowl. It is a poor place for fish. Trout are not plentiful, and the other kinds—suckers and chubs—are soft and insipid.

The Carson River affords water for the irrigation of immense tracts of land in Douglas County, in Carson Valley, and other valleys below, and power for running many large quartz mills that work the ores of the Comstock Lode. The first of these mills are at Empire City, and they are thence found all along down the river to, and a short distance below, the town of Dayton.

Owing to the great quantities of water taken from it for the irrigation of ranches above in Carson Valley, the river becomes almost dry in the lower part of its course during the latter part of each summer. To remedy this evil large storage reservoirs should be constructed in the mountains and higher foot-hill regions.

WALKER RIVER.

Walker River rises in Mono and Alpine Counties, California, and flows through Douglas and Lyon Counties, Nevada. Walker Lake, Esmeralda County, forms its terminal sink. The river is about 150 miles in length. Its waters are bright and sweet, and are filled with trout and good food fishes of other varieties. The river has two large branches, known as the East and the West Walker, which unite below Mason's Valley. The waters of Walker River serve to irrigate immense tracts of as fine land as is to be found on the Pacific Coast, lying in Antelope, Smith's, and Mason's Valleys. For the first half of its course the river flows northward, then it suddenly turns south and forms Walker Lake. This lake is a very bright, beautiful, and picturesque sheet of water. It is very irregular in form, being frequently widened and contracted between its rocky shores. It is about thirty miles long and has a width of from five to eight miles.

THE OWYHEE.

The Owyhee is the only Nevada river that finds its way to the ocean. It rises in Elko County, in the northwestern corner of the State, and, flowing north into Idaho, becomes a tributary of the Snake River. Through the Snake its waters find their way north into the Columbia River, and thence into the Pacific Ocean.

Every spring salmon ascend the Owyhee and afford the anglers of Tuscarora and other mining towns and camps in that part of the State excellent and profitable sport. The Owyhee irrigates many beautiful valleys. In this region prairie-chickens and sage-hens are abundant, and a few deer are also found. In the vicinity of the river are fine and extensive cattle ranges.

REESE RIVER.

Reese River takes its rise in the Toyabee Range of mountains, in Nye County, near the center of the State. It runs through Lander County, near Austin, and continues its course northward (under-ground and on the surface) to near the Humboldt River, where it disappears in the tule marsh. Strictly speaking, it "empties" nowhere in particular. It has a channel that leads into the Humboldt a short distance below Argenta, but in summer its waters fall short of reaching that stream by twenty miles. Although Reese River is a narrow and shallow stream, it has a length of about 150 miles. There are many fine valleys and much excellent grazing land on the bordering benches and hills.

OTHER RIVERS.

Other so-called rivers in Nevada are Quin River, a large creek which rises in Idaho and runs south in Humboldt County to a small terminal "sink" situated at the north end of a great range of mud flats and marshes that lie to the northward of Pyramid Lake. There are good stock ranges in the Quin River country. The Rio Virgin is a small stream about eighty miles in length situated in Lincoln County, in the extreme southeastern part of the State. It takes its rise in Utah and empties into the Colorado River. It has a tributary of considerable rise called Muddy Creek, or the "Big Muddy," on and about which is much excellent land and several deserted Mormon villages. At one time there were 500 Mormon families settled in this part of Nevada, but they were called back to Salt Lake by Brigham Young, and abandoned their comfortable homes and fine and fertile farms. The mouth of the Rio Virgin is but 800 feet above the level of the sea, all this region being in what is known as the "Colorado Basin." The climate is much the same as that of Los Angeles, California. Oranges, figs, lemons, almonds, olives, pomegranates, and all other semi-tropical fruits grow to perfection; also cotton and tobacco. All the grains, vegetables, and fruits of the temperate zone flourish finely. This spot is the Eden of the great basin region.

The Colorado River forms the southeastern boundary of Nevada. Although it is not one of the rivers of the State system, yet it is one to which Nevada has some claim. Where it sweeps along the southern border of the State the stream is half a mile wide and has a depth of from ten to twenty feet. The river is navigable for steamboats from Callville, a short distance between the mouth of the Rio Virgin, to Port Isabel, on the Gulf of California, a distance of 600 miles. Callville is one of the towns (now almost deserted) founded by the Mormons during their occupation of that region of the country. The proposed railroad from Salt Lake City would cause this region to again become populous and prosperous.

Mineral Treasures of Nevada.

There are mines of the precious metals in every county in the State. There are mines of gold, silver, lead, copper, and other valuable metals in all the rugged, parallel ranges of mountains running through the great central plateau. Mining and agriculture are thus pursued side by side. Lying between the mountain ranges and running in the same direction are valleys containing arable land, while on the benches and lower hills are excellent grazing lands, on which grow nutritious bunch-grass and other valuable native grasses. In all parts of the State mining is being profitably pursued, and almost weekly new and valuable discoveries of the precious metals are somewhere being made. Although the country has been walked and ridden over in various directions for the past twenty-five years, there are still hundreds of sections where no real prospecting has ever been done. Even in the oldest and best-known mining camps, many discoveries yet remain to be made. Although explorations were made in the southern half of the State in the early days, and thousands of mining locations made, little real mining has been done on any of the hundreds of large and promising veins discovered. The work done has been mere surface scratching, and the majority of the claims have long since been abandoned by their locators. Lack of facilities for the transportation of ores and supplies made it impracticable to work mines situated at a great distance from lines of railroad. The men who prospected and made locations in wild and distant regions were men of little means, and when their small stocks of money and provisions were exhausted, they were obliged to abandon their claims and return to the settlements, as men of capital could not be induced to invest their money in mines out in the wilderness far from any means of transportation. Thus it happens that there are many sections of the country the mines of which are the same as unprospected —mines which will produce millions when lines of railroad shall furnish facilities for the transportation of ore, machinery, and supplies. In Lincoln, Nye, White Pine, Lander, Elko, and Humboldt Counties, there are hundreds of mining districts in which this is the case, and in these hundreds of districts are lying unworked thousands of quartz veins, all showing more or less of the precious metals at the very surface, and even in the croppings above the surface.

A thousand years of mining will not exhaust the mineral treasures of the mountains of Nevada. Cheaper and cheaper means of mining and reducing ores will continue to be found, and presently it will be possible to work the mines of common metals which cannot now be touched. Besides gold and silver the mountains of Nevada contain veins of copper, lead, iron, antimony, nickel, zinc, and many others, as cobalt, graphite, and the like. Not only are the mountains of the State rich in all kinds of metals, but the lower lands are also filled with valuable mineral treasures. In the basins of extinct lakes in all parts of the State, and aggregating hundreds of square miles, are inexhaustible deposits of borax, soda, salt, gypsum, glaubers, alum, sulphur, and many other mineral products of a similar character, which are only now beginning to be utilized at points near lines of railway.

Agricultural Resources.

In the limited space at command in a small book such as this it is not possible to more than give to the agricultural and horticultural resources of the State a passing glance, as has been done in the case of the mining and mineral products and resources. Although until within a very few years past Nevada has never been thought of outside of the State as being anything else than a region of mines, of metals, and beds of minerals, it is now evident that she has agricultural advantages and resources long unsuspected. Nevada is well calculated to become a great stock-growing State. Already she has her "cattle kings," and they are not as the roving cattle kings of other lands. They have struck their roots deep in the soil and are permanent residents. While the tillage of the soil alone will be found as profitable here as elsewhere for the small farmer whose ranch is within reach of a ready market, the real and great business of the Nevada land owner must be stock-growing. This is not a matter of choice or taste, but is a thing demanded by the configuration of the country, the climate, and the nature of the soil. In order that the natural resources of the country may be properly utilized the greater part of the valley regions (nearly all at a distance from towns) must be given up to the stock-grower. He must have valley lands on which to raise sufficient hay and other feed to tide his live-stock through any severe spells of cold weather or big snow-storms that may occur during the winter months. In order to utilize the vast surrounding grazing ranges the cattle king must have a "center stake" driven in some good, productive valley. This is required as a magazine of supplies for the winter season. While cattle, horses, and sheep will find a living on the ranges during the greater part of the winter, still the stock-grower who would not suffer occasional disaster must be provided against the accident of possible cold "snaps" and unusually heavy snow-falls. A glance over the physical features of the country shows that the proportion of arable to grazing land is very well balanced. When proper attention shall be given to the storage of water for irrigation it will be found that each valley will have sufficient capacity to produce hay, grain, and root crops adequate to the requirements of the flocks and herds that can find pasturage on the surrounding range.

On the ranges are found several valuable native grasses, some of which are cut for hay. Those most valuable for hay are the blue-joint, red-top, one variety of bunch-grass, and several varieties of clover. All these grasses grow in the moist lands of the valleys and natural meadows, but some varieties of bunch-grass flourish on the hills and elevated benches. Among the native grasses of the country could no doubt be found one valuable variety at least that would grow without irrigation and that could be greatly improved by cultivation. Such a grass is probably that called "sand-grass," of which large fields are frequently seen in dry, sandy, and apparently utterly barren plains. It grows to a height of about fifteen inches and has many spreading branches on each stalk, which branches are loaded with a large black seed, that is very fattening, and of which all kinds of grazing animals are very fond. It would be well to sow the seed of this grass, which is a species of bunch-grass, on properly plowed and prepared ground in order to ascertain its capability of cultivation. There are not fewer than forty varieties of native grasses found in Nevada and eight or ten kinds of clover. Alfalfa is the forage plant most cultivated for hay, and on a suitable soil has no superior. Timothy, red and white clover, and other tame grasses, do well.

A very valuable native forage plant, for the reason that it flourishes in even the most arid and sterile localities, is that commonly called "white sage." It is a plant of a whitish-ash color and does not belong to the "artemesia," or sagebrush, family. This hardy plant furnishes good winter feed for cattle. It is resinous and bitter until after the heavy frosts of early winter. Freezing renders it tender, sweet, and nutritious. Even human beings may support life on the white-sage. In hard winters, before the whites came into the country, at times when no game could be found, the Piutes were occasionally obliged to subsist for weeks at a time wholly on white sage cooked by boiling it in baskets by means of hot stones.

The Comstock Mines.

Having now given the reader some idea of the topography and physical aspect of the State, with a hasty general view of its mineral and agricultural productions and resources, we shall give a more particular account of the Comstock Lode, in which the first discovery of silver was made; where the deepest shafts have been sunk, and where mining for the precious metals is to be seen on a grander scale than anywhere else in the United States, or anywhere in the New World, taking into consideration the power of the machinery used and the examples of scientific mining engineering to be seen. A description of the mines and mining methods of the Comstock will answer for those of all other parts of the State, except that in places where the ores are argentiferous galena, or otherwise very base, smelting furnaces take the place of the ordinary stamp and pan mills.

The Discovery of Silver.

The discovery of silver in Nevada in 1859 (then Western Utah), caused an immense excitement in California, and indeed throughout the United States. The excitement was one such as had not been before seen since the discovery of the gold mines of California. Permanency and ultimate value being considered, the discovery of silver undoubtedly deserves to rank in merit above the discovery of the gold mines of California, as it gives value to a much greater area of territory and furnishes employment to a much larger number of persons. It has given wealth and population to all the vast region lying between the Sierra Nevada and the Rocky Mountain Ranges.

Gold was first discovered in this region in the spring of 1850. It was found in what is now known as Gold Canyon, by a company of Mormon emigrants *en route* to California. Having arrived too early to cross the Sierras, they encamped on the Carson River, where the town of Dayton now stands, to await the melting away of the snow on the mountains. To while away the time some of the men of the party tried prospecting in a large canyon that put into the river near their camp. They found gold in the first pan of gravel they washed. Looking further they soon found that certain bars and gravel banks afforded much richer pay dirt than that first tried. They were able to make from $5.00 to $8.00 a day, but left as soon as the mountains were passable, as they anticipated taking out gold by the pound on reaching California. Other emigrants who followed the Mormons did some mining in the canyon while camped on the river. All made good wages, and one or two families stopped and went regularly to work at mining. However, when the supply of water in the canyon gave out toward the end of summer, they " pulled up stakes " and crossed the mountains to California.

What was told of the mines on Gold Canyon by these emigrants induced parties of miners working in and about Placerville to visit them. During the winter and spring months, while there was water, these men were able to make from half an ounce to an ounce a day. The camp had no permanent population, however, until the winter and spring of 1852–53, when there were over 200 men at work on the bars and gravel banks along the canyon, with rockers, toms, and sluices.

As the gold found in the canyon came from quartz veins toward its head, about Silver City and Gold Hill, these early miners were even then on the track of the great Comstock Lode, but without once even suspecting the existence of such a large and rich veins The trading-post, or little hamlet near the junction of the canyon and the Carson River, which at first served as a base of supplies, was presently left far behind as the miners worked their way up the stream from bar to bar, and they founded a town of their own, on a plateau near the canyon, called Johntown. This town was situated a short distance below where Silver City now stands, and was then the "mining metropolis" of Western Utah. One dilapidated stone chimney yet stands as a monument to mark the site of this now ruined mining town.

Johntown constituted a center from which prospectors occasionally scouted forth. These prospectors had no thought of anything except placer mines— native gold in gravel deposits. In 1857 some of these Johntown miners struck paying gravel in Six-mile Canyon. This canyon is about five miles north of Gold Canyon, for the greater part of its course, but the heads of the two canyons are only about a mile apart, and both are on what is now known as the Comstock Lode. The pay found on Six-mile Canyon began only about a mile below the massive croppings that tower above the Comstock; still these early miners never once thought of going up to the head of the ravine to look for and prospect the quartz veins; all they thought of was free gold in deposits of earth and gravel.

In January, 1859, James Finney, or Fennimore, better known by his popular *soubriquet* of "Old Virginia" (he being a native of the State of Virginia), John Bishop, and a few others of the Johntown miners, struck a rich deposit of free gold in placer diggings in a little hill at the head of Gold Canyon. From this hill the town of Gold Hill derives its name. These mines were so rich that most of the Johntown people moved to them. The gold was in a deposit of decomposed quartz mingled with soil, and the miners were really delving in a part of the Comstock Lode without at first knowing that they were at work on any quartz vein. These diggings yielded gold by the pound, at times.

In the spring of 1859 several Johntowners returned to the diggings they had discovered on Six-mile Canyon two years before. With these men went Peter O'Riley and Patrick McLaughlin, but finding all the paying ground already claimed they went to the head of the canyon and began prospecting on the slope of the mountain with a rocker, leading in a small stream of water from a neighboring spring. They found but poor pay in the light top dirt they were working (for there was no washed gravel), and they had about concluded to abandon their claim when they made the grand discovery of the age. They had sunk a small pit in which to collect water for use in their rockers. It was deeper than they had yet dug. Seeing in the bottom of this hole material of a different appearance from any they had yet worked, they were tempted to try some of it in their rocker. When a bucket of this dirt was rocked out, to their great delight the two men saw that they had made a "strike." The whole apron of their rocker was covered with a layer of bright and glittering gold.

In that little prospect hole, silver mining in America, as now known, was born. At that moment the eyes of these two men, standing alone among the sagebrush of the rugged mountain slope, rested upon the first of many hundreds of millions in the two precious metals that have since been taken out of the Comstock Lode; for in the rocker along with the gold was a quantity of rich black sulphuret of silver. This "heavy black stuff," which not a little puzzled the two uneducated miners, was almost pure silver. They thought it was some worthless base metal, and were very sorry to see it, as it clogged their rocker and interfered with the washing out of the fine gold-dust.

HENRY COMSTOCK.—Henry Thomas Paige Comstock, as he gave his name—has by many persons been credited with the discovery of the Comstock, but it is an honor to which he was not entitled. The credit of discovering silver in Nevada belongs to Peter O'Riley and Patrick McLaughlin. The grand discovery had been made several hours before Comstock knew of it. Toward evening on the day the "find" was made, Comstock, who had been out hunting his mustang, came to where the two men were at work. They were taking out gold by the pound and decomposed silver ore by hundreds of pounds. Comstock saw the gold and realized that a great strike had been made. He instantly determined to have a share. He at once declared that he had a claim upon the ground. He said he had located it some time before, also the water of the spring. He so blustered about his rights and so swaggered about what he could and would do that rather than have any trouble the two quiet miners agreed to take him in and give him a share of the mine.

No sooner had Comstock been made a partner in the mine than he placed himself at the front in every thing about it. He constituted himself superintendent, did all the talking and none of the working, and was always ready to tell strangers about the mine. When visitors came it was always *my* mine and *my* everything. Thus people came to talk of Comstock's mine and Comstock's vein; then it was the Comstock vein—as persons making locations asserted that they were on the same vein as Comstock, *i. e.*, the Comstock vein—and in that way the name of Comstock became fastened upon the whole lode. As the first claim was called the Ophir, that would have been a more fitting name for the whole vein than the one it now bears. For a long time Comstock no more appreciated the heavy black material that accompanied the gold, and in lumps of which much of the gold was embedded, than did O'Riley and McLaughlin. It was not until returns had been received from samples of it sent to California for assay that anyone in Nevada knew that the "heavy black stuff" was almost pure silver. With the returns of the assays came a rush from California. The assays were made at Nevada City, California, and the result so astonished the assayer that he could hardly believe his figures or his eyes. But other assays verified those first made, and the immense richness of the ore in both gold and silver could no longer be doubted. A few men were let into the secret, they let in a few more, and at once the great news spread far and wide. Soon miners, speculators, and adventurers of all kinds came over the Sierras to the silver mines in swarms. A town of tents, brush shanties, and canvas houses began to appear on the side of Mount Davidson—then known as "Sunrise Peak," as it caught the first rays of the morning sun. It was about the 1st of June when the silver was first struck, and, the weather being warm, many persons camped in the open air—cared for neither tent nor brush shanty.

There were about 1,000 persons in Western Utah at the time silver was discovered, and all were living under Mormon rule. Most of those in the country at that time were engaged in farming and cattle growing, in trade with the emigrants, or in gambling and running off stock; only about 200 were engaged in mining, and all these were working gold placers. A number of ranchers from surrounding valleys took up claims on the line of the lode when they heard that it was a silver vein, but neither the placer miners, the ranchers, nor any one else that was in the country at the time the great discovery was made, ever got more than a few hundreds or thousands of dollars out of it.

The Fate of the Discoverers.

Although Comstock was not a discoverer, he was one of the original locators on the lode. He sold his interest for $10,000. With this he opened a store in Carson City for the sale of such goods as the trade of the country demanded; also a similar store, but with a smaller stock, at Silver City. Knowing nothing of business, having no education, and being unable to keep books, he was soon "flat broke." After losing all the property he possessed in Nevada, Comstock struck out into Idaho and Montana, where he prospected for some years without success. In September, 1870, while encamped near Bozeman, Montana, *en route* to prospect in the Big Horn country, he committed suicide, blowing out his brains with his six-shooter.

PATRICK McLAUGHLIN sold his interest in the Ophir (the discovery claim) for $3,500, which sum he soon lost, and he then worked as a cook at the Green mine, in the southern part of California, for a time. He finally died while wandering from place to place and working at odd jobs, generally as a cook.

PETER O'RILEY held his interest until it brought him about $50,000, a part of which he received in the shape of dividends. He erected a stone hotel on B Street, Virginia City, called the Virginia House. He then began dealing in mining stocks and soon lost everything. Under the guidance of spirits—he was a

Spiritualist—he finally began running a tunnel into a bald and barren granite spur of the Sierras, near Genoa, in Douglas County, expecting to strike a richer vein than the Comstock. However, the spirits talked so much to him about caverns of gold and silver that he became insane and was sent to a private asylum at Woodbridge, California, where he soon died.

The men who made millions were those who came after the mines had been pretty well prospected, as Mackay, Fair, Sharon, Jones, and others.

Early Mining and Milling.

Once people became convinced of the richness, extent, and permanency of the ore deposits on the Comstock, towns were built up on the lode and at points in the valleys as if by enchantment. Machinery was brought over the Sierras under all manner of difficulties by teams, and soon mills for working the ores were built by scores. In 1859 the Americans, as a people, knew nothing about silver mining. At that time there were probably not a dozen American miners on the Pacific Coast who had ever even seen a sample of silver ore. In the California placer mines, however, were quite a number of Mexicans who had worked in silver mines in their own country. These men at once deserted their gold placers in California and came flocking over to the Sierras when the cry of "Plata! mucha plata!" was raised among them. "A gold placer," said they, "is soon worked out, but a silver mine lasts for generations and generations."

At first the word of the Mexicans was law in the new silver mines, both as regarded ore and the methods of mining and working it. Every American miner endeavored to secure a Mexican partner, or at least a Mexican foreman to take charge of his mine. Mexican methods, however, soon proved to be too slow for the Americans. Their arastras, patios, and little adobe smelting furnaces were the primitive contrivances of a non-mechanical people, and of a race of miners working as individuals, and on a very small scale at that.

The Americans at once introduced stamp mills for crushing the ore, and next introduced pans to hasten the process of amalgamation. The operation of amalgamating the crushed ore, which required days by the patio process, was reduced to hours by the use of steam-heated iron pans.

The Mexican miners were no better underground at working in the vein than they were on the surface, at extracting the precious metals after the ore was mined. In the Mexican mine, where everything was managed according to their own notions—the owner being a Mexican named Gabriel Maldanado—they carried the ore out of the mine in rawhide sacks, the miners climbing to the surface by means of a series of notched poles. Their timbering was also very defective. In ore bodies so large as those of the Comstock, they did not know how to support the ground.

Among the miners working in the gold placers of

California at the time of the discovery of silver on this side of the Sierras, were a few Germans who had worked in the silver mines of their "Vaterland," and among these were some half dozen who had been educated in the mining academy of Freyberg, and had received regular scientific and practical training in the art of mining. The mining and metallurgical knowledge of these men was the best then existing in any part of the world, as regarded the working of argentiferous ores. The Germans introduced the barrel process of amalgamation and the roasting of ores. While the barrel process was a great improvement on the patio, it was found not so well adapted to the rapid working of the Comstock ores as the newly invented pan process. It has also been found that the free milling ores of the lode do not require to be roasted.

Philip Deidesheimer, a German who had been appointed superintendent of the Ophir Mine, however, invented a method of timbering in "square sets," which is perfect in every respect, and which is still in use in all Comstock mines. By this method of building up squares of framed timbers an ore vein of any width may be safely worked to any height or depth; a vein 300 feet in width may as rapidly be worked as one only 10 or 20 feet wide.

Mining Difficulties and Inventions.

Early in the mining history of the Comstock there began to be heavy flows of water with which to contend. This called for pumping machinery and apparatus; and as greater and greater depth was attained, larger and larger pumps were demanded. The best and heaviest machinery in use in Europe was examined, and upon this improvements were from time to time made as increased flows of water required increased capacity. All the inventive genius of the Pacific Coast was called into play, and the result has been the construction of some of the most powerful and effective steam and hydraulic pumping apparatus to be found in any part of the world.

At first the water with which the Comstock miners had to contend was cold, but it was not long before the deeper workings cut into parts of the vein where were tapped heavy flows of hot water—water actually hot enough to cook an egg, or to scald a man to death almost instantly. Several miners have lost their lives by falling into large tanks, or sumps, of this water, hot from the vein. The hot water called for fans, blowers, and all kinds of ventilating apparatus, as men working in heated drifts had to have a supply of cool and fresh air sent in to them. Great improvements have also been made in hoisting cages, though the first idea of these came from Europe.

In California at the time of the discovery of the Comstock, were many men who had worked in the mines of Cornwall, England. These men thoroughly understood all manner of under-ground work, and were able to successfully carry through many undertakings in the way of sinking shafts, inclines, and winzes, and in making raises and running drifts in ground where the difficulties at first sight seemed almost insurmountable.

Various Mining and Milling Appliances.

Compressed air for running power drills, and for driving fans and small hoisting engines at depths varying from 1,000 to 3,000 feet below the surface, was early adopted in the Comstock mines, as also were the several new explosives for blasting. Diamond drills for drilling long distances through solid rock were also at one time in general use, but have been discarded for prospecting purposes, being found unreliable. The existence of ore may be ascertained by means of the diamond drill, but the amount found is a matter of uncertainty in all cases.

By the pan processes in the early days there were immense losses in the precious metals and in quicksilver. While the pans might be much alike in construction almost every millman was making experiments with some secret process of his own for the amalgamation of the ore. It now seems ridiculous, but some millmen were actually using sagebrush tea in their pans, and others a decoction of cedar bark. They tried all manner of trash, both mineral and vegetable. It was at that time that untold millions in gold, silver, and quicksilver were swept away into the Carson River with the tailings; for the ore on which all these experiments were tried was almost pure silver. Although scores of amalgamating pans of various patterns have been invented and patented, there is still room for improvement. The improvements made from time to time have resulted in saving a large per cent of the precious metals contained in the ores operated upon, and also in a smaller loss of quicksilver, yet none of the apparatus in use is perfect. Experiments having in view further savings are still constantly being made.

The Comstock as a School for Miners.

The Comstock is the mother of silver mining in America. In this lode hundreds of men have obtained a thorough practical knowledge of mining in all its forms and departments. Men who were graduated on the Comstock are now to be found in all parts of the world. They early went to Idaho, Montana, Utah, Colorado, New Mexico, Arizona, Alaska, and British Columbia. Old Comstock foremen and superintendents are to-day in charge of mines in Mexico, Central America, South America, Australia, Africa, China, Japan, and all other regions where there is mining for the precious metals. Already they are in the gold fields of the Amoor River—having pushed their way across from Alaska—and they are ready to push their way to the ends of the earth in search of the precious metals.

Virginia City and its Surroundings.

Virginia City, the county seat of Storey County, is situated on the eastern face of Mount Davidson, the culminating peak of a range of rocky hills running northeast and southwest, and having a length of about thirty-two miles. Mount Davidson rises to a height of 7,775 feet above the level of the sea, and is a rocky, treeless peak. On the slope of this mountain, about 1,775 feet below its summit, lies Virginia City. It may be said that the city occupies a position about midway between the base and the apex of the mountain, as the Carson River, which flows along near the eastern foot of the range, is 1,700 feet below the town. It is literally " a city set on a hill."

From the tents and brush shanties set up near the Ophir Mine immediately after the discovery of silver was made, the growth of the town was rapid. The first structure worthy of the name of "house" was erected in the summer of 1859, by Lyman Jones, a pioneer miner of Gold Canyon. It was of canvass and was 18x40 feet in size. Soon several frame structures were removed from Johntown and from Dayton (then called "Chinatown") to the " new diggings" of " Ophir." Lumber from saw-mills in the foot-hills of the Sierras was then procured and a few small houses and offices erected. As there was then no wagon road up the mountain to where the city now stands it was necessary to carry lumber up to the new diggings on horses, half packing and half dragging it from the valley, where it was delivered by wagons. Very soon, however, a wagon track was made up the mountain, and building then progressed more rapidly.

At first the new mining camp had no fixed or acknowledged name. It was variously spoken of as "Ophir," "Ophir Diggings," "Pleasant Hill," and "Mount Pleasant Point," though at that time there could have been nothing very "pleasant" about the place, except the sight of the gold and silver then being dug out by the pound and by the ton almost at the surface of the ground—less than a yard below the roots of the sage-brush. Even as late as October, 1859, the place was called Ophir Diggings. About that time James Fennimore, known among the miners as "Old Virginia," was in the camp one night, having a "little run with the boys," when he fell and broke his whisky bottle against a rock. Old Virginia picked up the bottom part of the bottle, in which still remained a small quantity of the precious liquid, and, solemnly pouring it upon the ground, said, "I christen this camp Virginia!" He called upon those present to bear witness to the fact that he had duly named and christened the town in honor of himself and his native State.

Old Virginia was a favorite among the miners, and one and all declared that Virginia should be the name of the town. At first the place was called "Virginia Town," but soon the word city was tacked on to Virginia, the name by which it was christened, and Virginia City it has remained. Old Virginia had some right to name the town. He was one of the first to mine on Six-mile Canyon, working at a point now included in the eastern suburbs of the city, and he was the first man in the country to locate a quartz vein in the vicinity. This vein was a large one lying west of the Ophir, and known as the "Virginia Vein," or "Virginia Croppings." This back lead contained a vast deal of "base metal," but very little paying ore. The location was made February 22, 1858, more than a year before the discovery of silver. In July, 1861, "Old Virginia" was thrown from a "bucking" mustang, in the town of Dayton, and killed. At the time of his death he was possessed of about $3,000 in gold coin.

The first buildings were erected pretty much at random in the new town, but soon streets were laid out. Those nearest the Ophir Mine were first built on—A and B Streets. In the spring of 1860, B Street was the principal business street of the town, and there were several places of business on A Street, while many new buildings were going up on C Street —the principal business street at present.

The first winter (1859-60) many persons lived in holes excavated in the side of the mountain and roofed with sagebrush and earth. There were then no hotel accommodations worthy of the name. Peter O'Riley's stone hotel, on B Street, was not yet completed, and the International Hotel, owned by Bateman & Paul, was a little frame structure, capable of accommodating only a small number of persons, and those in the roughest style imaginable. In May, 1860, a war broke out with the Piute Indians that lasted a month. This trouble caused a grand stampede of the white settlers, and gave the new town a temporary backset, but the people soon recovered from their fright, and in another month building was as lively as before the war broke out.

During the years 1860-61 the town built up very rapidly, and in 1862-63 brick and stone "fire-proof" buildings were erected in all directions, as already fires began to be of frequent occurrence. Year by year the city grew in area, population, and wealth. Building went on both summer and winter, and at times was pushed almost day and night. As the mines were opened and worked their immense richness attracted hundreds and thousands of persons from California, and all parts of the Atlantic States and Canada. Money was more plentiful and the prices paid for skilled and all other kinds of labor were far higher than anywhere else on the American continent; all articles of merchandise also brought greater prices than could anywhere else be obtained. Gold coin jingled in the pockets of all in the city— those of the drones as well as those of the workers.

With the honest, industrious, and peaceable came the sharper, the idler, and the desperado. Adventurers of every class and every grade of wickedness, both male and female, swarmed in the town. There were many desperate affrays, robberies, and murders. "Cutting and shooting scrapes" were of almost daily and nightly occurrence in the streets and in the saloons. At one time the nightly killings were so frequent that residents expected each morning to hear that there was "a man for breakfast."

Finally murders, robberies, and incendiary fires became so frequent that a "Vigilance Committee," known as "601," was organized and became active in the spring of 1871. It was the object of the organization to rid the town of all manner of evil-doers, and particularly of such desperate characters as almost without provocation killed peaceable citizens. After there had been two or three hangings by "601," and after many bad characters had received "notices" to leave (which all at once obeyed), the city again became quiet and orderly.

CITY IMPROVEMENTS.

Owing to the steep slope of the mountain, the site of the town was by no means favorable, but, at great cost for grading, many fine, level streets were constructed. The principal streets were then filled in to the depth of a yard with waste quartz and other hard, flinty rock from the mines. This work was so well done that to this day the streets are hard, smooth, and dry. The Virginia Gas Company was early organized, and the streets and business houses lighted with gas. As early as 1862 a water company organized and brought a supply of water from several tunnels run into the Virginia Range west of the city. This water was conveyed to the town by means of wooden flumes and iron pipes, and distributed to customers throughout the place. The supply of water, however, at that time was not adequate to the requirements of the town, and the quality was poor, being much impaired by the deleterious minerals it held in solution. Mention of the present system of water works will be made in another place.

Meantime, while the town was building up, good wagon roads had been constructed in various directions at great cost. A number of fire companies had been organized (provided at first with hand engines, but afterwards with steamers), and Virginia City began to take on the appearance of a real "city," not only in the number and substantial character of the buildings, and swarms of people it contained, but also in the number of conveniences it afforded, its many societies, churches, schools, theaters, clubs, orders, and organizations, usually considered the necessary adjuncts and requirements of civilized and intelligent communities. There were also several daily and weekly newspapers, telegraph, express, and all other similar offices required by business and mining men, and by the people at large. Indeed, in 1875 the area of the city was as great as at present, and much more populous, as at that time it was estimated to contain 20,000 people. Hundreds and thousands of these, however, were mere birds of passage, being neither business men nor owners of property. At and about Gold Hill at that time it was estimated that there

were about 10,000 souls. The two towns, originally a mile apart, were connected by buildings—had grown together. Both towns were filled with mills and mining works, that gave employment to many thousands of miners, mechanics, and workingmen of all grades and classes.

The Great Fire.

Everything was thus flourishing and prosperous—the "Big Bonanza" was yielding its millions, and several other mines were working great and rich bodies of ore—when Virginia City was overwhelmed by a great calamity.

On the morning of October 26, 1875, a fire broke out in a frame lodging-house on A Street, in the western part of the town, just above all the great business blocks, and in a few hours all in an area of half a mile square was laid in ashes. Before the fire was subdued no fewer than 2,000 buildings—including mills, hoisting works, churches, business houses, and structures of all kinds—were swept away. Hundreds of families were left homeless and destitute. Owing to the early hour at which the fire started (six o'clock), and the fearful rapidity with which it spread in all directions, few persons were able to save any of their goods or valuables. In all, property to the value of over $10,000,000 was destroyed. Many great and destructive fires had before swept through and devastated the city, but this was the greatest ever experienced in the place. Scores of buildings that had always been rated as fire-proof melted away in the fervent heat like frost in the rays of the morning sun.

Almost in the start the court-house, the building of the Washoe Club, the International Hotel, and several other large buildings, were ignited and began vomiting pillars of flame that scattered sparks and cinders far and wide. As the fire progressed the millions of feet of lumber and timbers and the thousands of cords of wood about the mining works made fires that could not be successfully combated, and which nothing could withstand. At the Consolidated Virginia Hoisting Works and Mill alone there were on fire at the same moment, and in one mass, 1,250,000 feet of lumber and timbers, and 800 cords of pine wood, not to speak of the two great buildings, and all the stores they contained; also the adjoining assay office, and contents. Across the street the freight and passenger depots of the Virginia and Truckee Railroad Company were sending up immense pillars of flame, while just south Piper's Opera House, an immense frame structure filled with all manner of very imflammable material, was a volcano, vomiting destruction on all sides. Between and about these large structures a score or more of smaller buildings were belching flames. This was the scene at but one spot. A few rods to the southward three tall churches (Catholic, Methodist, and Episcopal) were sending tongues of flame into the very clouds, amid whole acres of smaller buildings that formed a tumultuous sea of fire. At the same time to the northward the Ophir works, with fifty smaller structures, were wrapped in flame. In the same fierce way the fire was raging over half a mile square of the very heart of the town. Although there were scores of narrow escapes, only two persons lost their lives in the fire, and two or three were afterwards killed by falling walls.

To rebuild the town at once was the universal determination. The insurance on the property destroyed amounted to $2,500,000 (the loss at the Bonanza Mines alone was $1,461,000), which was something to begin with; besides many persons whose property was destroyed had plenty of money left with which to rebuild. There was not a moment's delay. The next morning the work of clearing away ruins preparatory to putting up new buildings was begun in all parts of the city, water being thrown upon the red-hot bricks to so cool them that they could be handled. Rebuilding began the morning after the fire, and hardly ceased day or night until all the ground of the burnt district had been again covered. The big mining companies were especially active. Although engaged in rebuilding the mills and works destroyed, the Consolidated Virginia Mining Company paid its regular dividends of $10 a share in November and December, the two amounting to $2,160,000. In less than thirty days from the time of the fire new works replaced those destroyed by fire, and the machinery was in place and ore hoisted on Thanksgiving-day. In sixty days after the fire the business streets of the city were rebuilt, and with larger and finer structures than those that had been destroyed. The whole burnt district was so soon covered with new buildings that strangers arriving in the city looked about them in surprise and asked, "Where was your big fire?" That was a busy time on the Virginia and Truckee Railroad, no fewer than forty-five trains a day passing over the road during the great building rush. But for the railroad the city and mining works could not have been rebuilt that year.

Virginia City at Present.

Although Virginia City covers as much ground and contains larger and finer buildings than before the great fire, it is not so populous as in the old flush times of the "Big Bonanza." In those days every hotel and lodging-house was filled to overflowing; now most of those in the city are permanent inhabitants and property owners—those who formerly composed the grand army of "sports," adventurers, and idlers have gone to other fields. At present the city contains a population of only about 9,000 persons, but nearly all those now in the place have permanent homes and some legitimate and remunerative employment. As about one-fourth of the male population is constantly at work under-ground in the lower levels of the various mines, the streets do not present so thronged an appearance as those of a non-mining town containing the same number of inhabitants. The place, however, presents a very different appearance on a holiday when all the mining works are shut down and the miners are on the surface.

The first care of the people of the city after rebuilding the place was to guard against the recurrence of such a sweeping conflagration. A number of huge water tanks were constructed high above the town on the side of the mountain, with a proper system of mains and hydrants extending through all parts of the city. The pressure is so great at' these hydrants that the firemen are able to throw a stream over the flag-staff of the tallest building in the city through a nozzle of the largest size. A few paid firemen now fight all the fires that occur in the city. As the hydrants are always ready the firemen have only to get to them, attach their hose, and at once they have powerful streams steadily playing on the fire. "Promptness of action" is their motto. They seldom allow a fire to get out of the building in which it originates. Usually they have a fire out before a steam fire-engine could get up steam.

The fire mains are distinct from those which supply water for domestic purposes, and those again from such as furnish water for use at the mills and hoisting works of the mines. There is a system of gates whereby the water may be shut off from the hydrants of any block in the city and turned to any other block or blocks of buildings. This system is so perfect that employes of the water company working in conjunction with the firemen are able to at once turn the water to any part of the city in which it may be required, at the same time shutting it off from all other parts.

All the churches, halls, district court-house, theater, and other public buildings are finer than those destroyed in the big fire, and again are seen trees and grounds of handsome appearance in various parts of the city. In the city are several school-houses that cost from $20,000 to $60,000, besides which there are a number of private schools, and the fine school of the Sisters of Charity. There is also a hospital—St. Mary's, a commodious brick structure—under the charge of the Sisters, as well as a large and well-conducted county hospital. Both are located beyond the eastern suburbs in quiet and pleasant places. The halls belonging to the many societies and secret orders are elegant and costly. The city now has electric lights, two daily newspapers, and one weekly.

The mills and hoisting works are a striking and characteristic feature of the place. The immense waste dumps, high trestle-work car tracks, trains of ore cars on the railroad, clouds of black smoke belched from many tall stacks, trains loaded with wood and timber, all tell that mining is the great industry of the city; then much of the street talk heard is of mines and mining stocks.

The International Hotel is the oldest in the city.

It was founded in 1860, when it was a mere frame shanty fronting on B Street. The hotel destroyed by the big fire was a commodious brick structure, but the present building is far finer. It now extends from B to C Street, is constructed of brick, stone, and iron, and is six stories in height. It is capable of accommodating in excellent style a large number of guests.

Views from the City and Vicinity.

Though the landscape visible from the city cannot be called beautiful, yet it is grand and picturesque. On all sides except the east, the town is shut in by near ranges of high, rocky, and barren mountains. To the eastward the eye reaches over a vast area composed of tracts of sandy desert, valley lands, dark and rocky hills, and rugged and towering mountain ranges. The chief of these is the Humboldt Range, seen blue or purple in the distance, from 150 to 190 miles away. These mountains and their snow-clad peaks stand out against the dark-blue of the sky far beyond the green cottonwood groves that follow the meanderings of the Carson River, far beyond the Forty-mile Desert and the lake and sink of the Carson, and beyond Humboldt Lake and Sink.

To the northeast are seen several sharp and splintered peaks, while to the southeast, from twenty to fifty miles away, rise the huge and grand peaks of the Como Mountains. From the Divide (the dividing ridge between Virginia and Gold Hill) may be obtained a magnificent view of the main Sierra Nevada

Range and its many mighty snow-capped peaks as they trail and circle away from west to south till they are lost to view behind lower interior ranges at a point over 150 miles away.

The View from the Summit of Mt. Davidson.

From the peak of Mount Davidson may be obtained a grand and extensive view of the country in all directions. To the westward is seen Washoe Lake and the green meadows and fields by which it is surrounded. Although Washoe Valley and its lake seem to be just at the foot of the mountain they are from eight to ten miles distant. Beyond and high above the valley tower the pine-clad Sierras, with, along their line, several giant granite peaks, snow-capped the greater part of the year. Prominent among these stands out Bald Mountain, just north of Lake Tahoe, and within plain view Mount Lincoln, Job's Peak, Silver Mountain, and many other peaks that have names. Twenty miles to the northward are to be seen the green pastures and alfalfa fields of the Truckee Meadows, while to the southward we have the Sierra Range and Eagle and Carson Valleys. Carson City is hid by intervening low hills. To the eastward are the same deserts and mountains that compose the landscape viewed from the city, but from the top of the mountain the eye ranges over a vastly wider field.

The Virginia and Truckee Railroad.

From our elevated position on the peak of Mount

Davidson we may trace nearly the whole course of the Virginia and Truckee Railroad. This road runs from Reno to Virginia City *via* Carson City, and is fifty-two miles in length. Besides being in one part the most crooked railroad in the world, its whole course is a great curve. The distance from Virginia City to Reno as the crow flies is only about seventeen miles, and but twenty-two by wagon road, yet to connect the two points by rail required a road fifty-two miles in length.

From Reno, where the road connects with the Central Pacific, its course is southward through Truckee, Meadows, and Steamboat, Washoe and Eagle Valleys, to Carson City, a distance of thirty-one miles. From Carson City the road runs east down the Carson River about nine miles, when it leaves the river and, turning to the north, begins to climb the mountains to Virginia. From the river to Virginia the distance is thirteen miles and the maximum grade is 116 feet. In climbing the mountain there are many very short curves. The maximum radius of curves is 300 feet. By adding together all these curves it is found that a passenger on the road actually travels seventeen times round a circle between Virginia and Carson City. On the road are six tunnels, whose united length is 2,400 feet, and there are numerous deep cuts in very hard rock. The only high bridge is the trestlework on which the road crosses Crown Point Ravine, at Gold Hill. This bridge is eighty feet in height.

Ground was broken on the road February 19, 1869, and eight months thereafter the most difficult part of it was finished and trains were running to Carson—twenty-one miles. The construction of this twenty-one miles of road cost $1,750,000, the greater part of which sum was expended on the first thirteen miles. In round numbers the whole fifty-two miles cost $3,000,000. The road does an immense business in the transportation of Comstock ores to quartz mills on the Carson River, and in carrying back from the valley wood, lumber, and timbers for the mines; it also carries from Reno to Virginia great quantities of all kinds of goods and merchandise—coal, ice, provisions, fruit, and machinery—with mails, express, and many passengers daily. The road connects with the Carson and Colorado Road at Mound House, eleven miles below Virginia City. The road and its many side-tracks and switches constitute a lasting monument to the engineering skill of the late I. E. James.

The Days of "Bull Teams."

Before the Virginia and Truckee Railroad was built all freight was transported by teams. Ore was hauled to the mills by teams, and teams brought to the mines all the wood, lumber, and timber required. Teams also hauled over the Sierras all the mining machinery and supplies required by the mines and mills, and all the goods and merchandise needed by various kinds of stores, shops, and business houses.

When the Central Pacific was completed this hauling of merchandise was from Reno, *via* the Geiger grade wagon-road. Hundreds of teams of all kinds were required to handle the goods and merchandise, other hundreds the ore, wood, lumber, and timbers, and still others to do the miscellaneous hauling of the country. When the big reduction works of the Ophir Mining Company were in operation near Franktown, in Washoe Valley, lines of teams from one to three miles in length were to be seen moving along the Ophir grade. On all other roads it was much the same. Teams of from ten to sixteen horses or mules hauled trains of from two to four loaded wagons. At times so many teams thronged Virginia City that blockades occurred which could not be broken for hours. Stages, omnibuses, delivery wagons, drays, carts, buggies, carriages, and all kinds of vehicles were inextricably mingled in a jam that filled the principal streets for blocks. With all the cursing of "mule-punchers," "swampers," and "bull-teamsters," it would often be two or three hours before the wheels of traffic again began to revolve. When these blockades occurred about noon, teamsters would often get out their dinner pails, spread their meal on their load of wood, brick, or lumber, bring out from the nearest saloon a measure of beer, and in a leisurely way partake of the midday repast. Then all passengers and all mail and express matter were carried by stages, and so great was the rush of travel and business that the coaches went out and returned in droves, five and six in a string. In 1859, 1860, and 1861, great quantities of goods were transported across the Sierras from California on the backs of mules. Some of the pack-trains were composed of fifty, eighty, and even as many as one hundred mules. They brought over all kinds of freight, even huge casks of liquor and large pieces of mill machinery. On the return trip they often carried passengers. In those days the "hurricane deck" of a mule was not to be despised.

THE COMSTOCK SYSTEM OF WATER SUPPLY.

The Virginia City and Gold Hill Water Works.

When silver was first discovered on the Comstock, the flow of water from natural springs was sufficient to supply all the wants of the small communities then constituting the towns of Gold Hill and Virginia City. As the population increased, wells were dug in many places (distant from springs), and the domestic needs of many families were for a long time supplied by water-carts that peddled the water of both wells and springs. Presently the water of several tunnels added to the available stock, but as mills and hoisting works multiplied, the demand for water for use in steam boilers became so great that it was impossible to supply it without creating a water famine among the people of the two towns, now thousands in number, with hundreds of new arrivals every week. In this emergency the Virginia City and Gold Hill Water Company was formed. Outside of mining companies it is the oldest incorporation on the Comstock Lode. The only available supply of water at that time was that flowing from a few tunnels that had been run into the mountain above the city for mining purposes. This was collected by means of ditches and wooden flumes, and stored in large wooden tanks, whence it was distributed about the city through iron pipes. When this supply became insufficient, as it soon did, tunnels were run for the express purpose of tapping water. As these drained out the hills and failed, new ones were run in the range both north and south of the city for a distance of several miles.

Finally every device was exhausted, and the hills above the level of the city were thoroughly drained. It then became necessary to look to the main range of the Sierra Nevada Mountains. In those mountains was an inexhaustible supply of the purest and best water to be found in the whole world, but between the lakes, creeks, and sparkling fountains of the Sierras and the range on which stood Virginia City, lay Washoe Valley, an immense trough nearly 2,000 feet in depth. How to get water over such a depression was the question. Mr. H. Schussler, an engineer of great repute, and who had planned the Spring Valley Water Works of San Francisco, was brought to Nevada to view the situation. He said the deep valley could be crossed, and in the spring of 1872 surveys were made and an order given Eastern manufacturers for the construction of a large wrought-iron pipe. The first section of the big pipe was laid June 11, 1873, and the last on the twenty-fifth day of July of the same year.

THE BIG WATER PIPE.

The total length of the pipe is 7 miles and 134 feet. The pipe has an interior diameter of 12 inches, and is capable of delivering 2,200,000 gallons of water in twenty-four hours. The inlet of the pipe is on a spur from the main Sierra Nevada Range, and the outlet is on the crest of the Virginia Range of mountains. The pipe lies across the valley in the form of an inverted siphon. At the lowest point, the perpendicular pressure on the pipe is 1,720 feet, or about 800 pounds to the square inch. The inlet being 465 feet higher than the outlet, the water is forced through the pipe under tremendous pressure. The water is brought to the inlet from the sources of supply in two large covered flumes, and at the outlet end of the pipe is delivered into two large flumes, which carry it to Virginia City, a distance of twelve miles.

This pipe was constructed of sheets of wrought iron riveted together. Each section was fastened with three rows of rivets. At the point of greatest pressure the iron was five-sixteenths of an inch in thickness, but near the ends, upon the sides of the two opposite mountains, it tapered down to one-sixteenth of an inch. In the construction of the pipe there were used 1,150,000 pounds of rolled iron and 1,000,000 rivets, while 52,000 pounds of lead were used in securing the joints of the sections. At each joint the sections were inserted into cast-iron sleeves, and it was within these sleeves that the lead was used. The total weight of the sleeves was 442,500 pounds.

The first flow of water through this pipe reached Gold Hill and Virginia City on the evening of August 1, 1873, amid the greatest rejoicings of the people of both towns. Cannons were fired, rockets sent up, and bands of music paraded the streets. Never before in any part of the world had water been conveyed under a pressure so great; and it still remains the greatest. Previous to this, 910 feet was the greatest perpendicular pressure under which water had ever been carried through an iron pipe. This had been accomplished by Mr. Schussler, at Cherokee Flat, California.

Additional Great Pipes.

In 1875 the water company laid alongside the first pipe a second having an inside diameter of ten inches. This pipe is lap-welded, and, there being no friction of rivet heads upon the water, the flow through it is equal to that through the twelve-inch pipe,— 2,200,000 gallons every twenty-four hours.

Before 1875 the supply of water was obtained from creeks on the eastern slope of the mountains lying

ADDITIONAL GREAT PIPES.

east of Lake Tahoe, but in the year named, the water company pushed their main supply flumes through to Marlette Lake, which lies inside of the Tahoe basin. To do this it was necessary to run a tunnel 3,000 feet in length through the dividing ridge, or rim, of the Tahoe basin. The sheet of water known as Marlette Lake is almost entirely artificial, and owes its existence to a big dam—is in reality a large reservoir. The water covers an area of over 300 acres, and in the middle is about 40 feet deep. The reservoir holds 16,000,000,000 gallons of water.

The second pipe was laid under the supervision of Capt. J. B. Overton, Superintendent of the works of the water company, who also extended the flumes, constructed the tunnel through the mountain ridge, and made all the other improvements. In 1887 a third iron pipe of twelve inches inside diameter was laid across the valley alongside the first two. It was also a welded pipe and delivers much more water than either of the others. The inlet pressure has been raised on all three pipes, and they now deliver a total flow of about 10,000,000 gallons in twenty-four hours. In 1887, also, a branch flume was run to the northward (Marlette Lake lying to the southward) a distance of nine miles, which taps a number of creeks tributary to Lake Tahoe on the east and northeast sides. In the same year a reservoir capable of holding 20,-000,000 gallons was constructed on Hobart Creek, on the east side of the dividing ridge. In and near the city are reservoirs holding from 3,000,000 to 10,000,000 gallons, and a number of tanks along the side of Mount Davidson of from 60,000 to 80,000 gallons, capacity. The water is brought a distance of from twenty-five to thirty-seven miles, and the supply (aided by the several storage reservoirs) is ample for all present uses. The total cost of the works of the company has been about $2,500,000. Each of the three pipes has its separate inlet and outlet, from two flumes and into two flumes. Between the outlet and the city the water passes through a large storage reservoir.

THE SUTRO TUNNEL.

While there was a scarcity of water on the surface at Virginia City, there was a superabundance of it, both hot and cold, under-ground in all the mines. Levels were flooded so suddenly that oftentimes the miners narrowly escaped being drowned by the vast subterranean reservoirs that were unexpectedly tapped. Great delays in mining were caused by these floods, and to pump out the water that filled the lower levels cost immense amounts of money. Several tunnels from 1,000 to 5,000 feet in length were run into the mountain, but they were of only temporary utility, as the shafts of the mines were soon below their level. In order to overcome these water troubles, Adolph Sutro early conceived the idea of running an immense drain tunnel under the Comstock Lode from the lowest possible point. A survey was made by Mr. H.

Schussler, and work was commenced on the great drain tunnel (since known as the Sutro Tunnel) October 19, 1869. It starts at the edge of the valley of the Carson River, at a point nearly east of Virginia City, and has a length of 20,145 feet—nearly 4 miles. It taps the central parts of the Comstock Lode at a depth of about 1,650 feet. The tunnel is 16 feet wide and 12 feet high. Drain flumes are sunk in the floor and over these are two tracks for horse-cars. It required nearly eight years to construct the tunnel, and the total cost was about $4,500,000. Although the leading mines had their shafts down nearly 3,000 feet before the tunnel was finished, yet it was of great use, as it saved 1,600 feet of pumping.

From the main tunnel branches were run north and south along the east side of the vein for a distance of over two miles, with which the several companies connected by drain drifts from their mines. The flow of water through the tunnel has at times been over 10,000,000 gallons in twenty-four hours. Between the mouth of the tunnel and the Carson River there are 155 feet of fall, but it has never been utilized for driving reduction works. New connections are still being made with the tunnel for drainage. Though it never paid anything near what was anticipated by Mr. Sutro, the tunnel still brings in a snug sum annually. Last year (the fiscal year that ended February 29, 1888) the receipts for royalties amounted to $237,258.33. It costs a considerable amount annually to keep the main tunnel and branches in repair. This great drain at a depth of 1,600 feet below the surface allows of Pelton water wheels being set up in the shafts of the several mines and worked under immense pressure, there being a free discharge from the wheels. At the C and C shaft of the Consolidated California and Virginia, such wheels have been put in every 500 feet from the surface down to the Sutro Tunnel level. The water used on the first wheel on the surface, in the stamp-mill, is caught up, led to the shaft, and used on the second 500 feet below, and so on down to the tunnel level, the power being brought from wheel to wheel to the surface by means of a system of steel wire cables. Thus is transmitted to the surface the power developed by the whole series of wheels.

The Reduction Works of the Early Days.

In the early days the building of quartz-mills kept pace with the building up of the towns. As early as October, 1859, Logan & Holmes had a four-stamp horse-power mill in operation at Dayton, and Hastings & Woodworth had two water-power arastras at work, which reduced six tons of ore a day. This ore was not worked as silver ore. It was from the surface of the Comstock Lode, at Gold Hill, and was worked for gold only. In the spring of 1860 many mills for working silver ore began to be erected.

The First Silver Mill.

The first silver-mill that went into operation was

the "Pioneer," erected by Almarin B. Paul, on Gold Canyon, at the north end of Silver City, just below the Devil's Gate. It was a steam mill and contained twenty-four Howland rotary stamps and twenty-four amalgamating pans. The work of erecting the mill was commenced May 24, 1860, and it began work August 13, the same year. Some others have claimed the honor of starting the first quartz-mill in Nevada, but this was undoubtedly the first silver-mill. In it were operated the first silver amalgamating pans ever seen anywhere. The iron amalgamating pans were the result of experiments made by Almarin B. Paul before he began the erection of his mill. He thought the German barrel process and Mexican patio too slow, and began to make experiments with some small iron pans that had been in use at some of the quartz-mills in California for grinding and working the sulphurets saved by concentrating machines in working the quartz of the gold mines. The best of these was found to be the "Knox Improved Pan," in which was a false bottom that formed beneath the pan a steam-tight heating chamber. By the use of this kind of pan, and by treating the heated pulp with certain quantities of salt, sulphate of copper, and some other chemicals, before adding quicksilver, it was found that a charge (whatever amount of crushed silver ore the pan would hold) could be amalgamated in about three hours. The results obtained with Knox's Improved Pan were so satisfactory that Mr. Paul placed pans of that pattern in his new mill. Soon after a score of pans of different styles were invented, and to this day pans of new patterns are still being invented and patented.

The Coover & Harris Mill, Gold Hill, was the first mill in the country to start up with steam. It blew its steam whistle a day before that of Paul's "Pioneer" was heard, but it could not then be called a silver-mill as it was working gold quartz, the same as was worked, in October the year before, at Dayton, by Logan & Holmes and Hastings & Woodworth. The mill had a fifteen horse-power engine that drove an eight-stamp Howland rotary battery and crushed six tons of ore a day. At first it was a dry crusher, but soon Paul's Concentrators and Knox' pans were used. The Harris of the firm was Dr. E. B. Harris, now a resident of Virginia City.

The Many Mills of the Early Days.

Very soon after these first mills went into operation several others started up. By the spring of 1862 no fewer than eighty-one quartz-mills were at work, the majority of them on ore from mines situated on the Comstock Lode. These mills were located in Virginia City, on Six and Seven-mile Canyons, at Gold Hill, Silver City, Dayton, at Empire City, and all along the Carson River below that town; two or three near Carson City (on Clear Creek and Mill Creek), and a dozen or more about Washoe Valley and down toward Steamboat Valley. Many of these mills were of small capacity, having only from two to ten stamps, but there were already a few first-class reduction works, as regards capacity, though their methods and processes were defective. The reduction works of the Ophir Company, in Washoe Valley, cost $500,000, contained thirty-six stamps, were driven by an engine of 100 horse-power, and was capable of working 100 tons of ore a day. The Gould & Curry Mill then building on Six-mile Canyon was of still greater capacity, and the Land, Bassett, Winfield, Empire State, Central, Marysville, Trench, Swansea, Phœnix, Succor, Rock Point, Merrimac, Vivian, and several other mills, contained from fifteen to twenty-five stamps each. After the completion of the Virginia and Truckee Railroad the majority of the outside mills (mills to which it was necessary to transport ore, wood, and other supplies by wagon) were pulled down and removed to new mining camps in various parts of the State. The greater part of the ores of the Comstock were then reduced in steam mills near the mines or in water mills on the Carson River on the line of the railroad; and this is still the case.

We now have fewer mills than in the early days, but they are of greater average capacity, and are in every respect more effective than were those first erected. More ore is crushed to the stamp, and the time required for the amalgamation of the pulp has been very materially reduced. All the present mills are so constructed that there is very little handling of the ores operated upon, and labor-saving apparatus has been introduced into nearly every department. Even the old oil lamps are being thrown out of the mills and the electric light introduced.

REDUCTION WORKS OF THE PRESENT DAY.
Description of the Process of Working Comstock Silver Ore.

In speaking of the works at present in use for the reduction of silver ore, it will only be necessary to describe the process in use in one mill, as all work after the same system. Being the most recently erected, and quite perfect in all its arrangements, the new mill of the Nevada Mill and Mining Company, commonly called the Chollar Mill (as it stands near the Chollar old shaft), shall furnish the illustration necessary to an understanding of the method of working Comstock ores now generally in use. The mill covers nearly an acre of ground, and the machinery is at present (March, 1889) driven in part by a Pelton water wheel 11 feet in diameter, and in part by power electrically transmitted from the Sutro Tunnel level. The mill building stands in a depression near the head of a small ravine. Such a site was selected in order that from the time the ore enters the mill its course at each stage necessary to its complete reduction, shall be downward—that there shall be no lifting or hoisting of ore or pulp.

The mill stands a little over one hundred yards

south of the Chollar shaft. From the shaft the ore is run in the same cars in which it is hoisted from the mine directly into the upper story of the mill. It is there dumped through openings in the floor into the ore bins. Over these ore bins are placed in a slanting position iron bars three inches apart, forming screens called "grizzlies." Through these screens the fine ore falls into the bins, while the large lumps of rock roll down upon a floor in front of the rock-breaker, an apparatus that works much on the same principle as a lemon-squeezer. Between the jaws of this powerful machine the largest and hardest piece of quartz rock is at once chewed into fragments sufficiently small to be fed into the batteries, where the heavy stamps reduce it to pulp. The ore is delivered into the batteries by self-feeders, which are so regulated as to keep constantly under the stamps the proper quantity of rock to do well the most work. At the Chollar (or Nevada) Mill there are sixty stamps, —twelve batteries of five stamps each. Each stamp weighs about eight hundred pounds. On the end of each stamp is a heavy head or block of iron or steel called a "shoe," and in the bottom of the mortar (a long iron box in which the stamps of each battery work) is a similar block of iron called a "die," upon which the shoe of the stamp strikes when it pulls. It is between these two blocks of steel that the quartz is crushed.

A small stream of water flows into each battery, and

as the ore is reduced to a powder the water floats it out through the fine screens that are fitted into the face of each mortar. The pulverized ore and water, on passing through the screens, falls into a small trough, or sluice, which carries the muddy mixture down to the settling tanks, on a floor below, in the amalgamating room. In the tanks the crushed ore settles and the water runs off. From the tanks the pulverized ore, which resembles thin mortar, is shoveled out upon the floor alongside the amalgamating pans, into which it is shoveled whenever they are to receive a fresh charge of ore.

The pans are of iron and each holds a " charge" of about 3,000 pounds of the mortar-like pulp. In the bottom of each pan are thick plates of chilled iron or steel called " dies," while revolving upon these are other heavy pieces of steel, called " shoes" or mullers. In the pans the pulverized ore is ground till it is much finer than when it passed through the screens of the battery.

When a pan has received its charge of pulverized ore ("pulp") a small amount of water is added to render it sufficiently thin to be readily stirred by the mullers. The pans have tight covers and double bottoms. The double bottoms are steam chambers by means of which the pulp in the pan is kept hot while it is ground and agitated. After a charge has been ground about two hours, some 300 pounds of quicksilver are added (for 3,000 pounds of pulp), also a certain quantity of salt and sulphate of copper; and sometimes soda or caustic potash and other chemicals, if thought necessary, when the agitation in the pan is continued two hours longer. The time of working in the pan varies from three to five hours.

The Chollar Mill has thirty of these pans. On a platform below that on which stand the pans are fifteen settlers. These are about twice the size of the pans. At the end of three or five hours each settler has drawn off into it the contents of two pans. In the settler the pulp, quicksilver, and amalgam are kept in motion for about two hours. During this time water is let in and the pulp made very thin. The quicksilver and amalgam settle to the bottom of the "settler," and are drawn off through a pipe and pass into a strainer—a strong canvas bag. There is an iron box around each strainer, and this is kept locked.

It is in the pan that amalgamation takes place. There the sulphuret and chloride of silver is changed to the metallic form by the chemical action of the sulphate of copper (bluestone) and salt, and when it takes the metallic form it at once unites with quicksilver. The gold contained in the ore (generally one-third of its whole value) being always in the metallic form, is amalgamated as soon as it is ground out of its inclosing shell of quartz, or pyrites of iron.

The thinned pulp—mere muddy water in appearance—on leaving the settlers passes into large wooden tubs called "agitators," in which are revolving rakes.

In these tubs is caught some valuable material—principally amalgam and quicksilver. From the "agitators" the pulp flows out of the reduction works through a small flume which conducts it to the blanket sluices, fifty yards away in the open air. The blanket sluices are broad, shallow flumes in the bottom of which are placed strips of coarse woolen blanketing. In passing over these blankets the pulp deposits pulverized iron pyrites containing gold, some fine particles of amalgam, and quicksilver; also such silver sulphurets as escaped being amalgamated in the pans. From time to time the blankets are taken out of the sluices and rinsed in a large tank, in which operation is saved whatever of value they may have caught.

The amalgam collected in the strainers standing below the settlers is placed in a press and as much quicksilver as possible pressed out, when it is placed in retorts, which are heated till all the mercury is driven off. There then remains behind the silver and gold, in a dull, rough-looking mass. This "crude bullion" is then broken up and placed in the melting pots, to be made into "bricks" and assayed. The bars or bricks made weigh about 100 pounds each. From the top and bottom of each pot or crucible of molten gold and silver is taken a small quantity of the fluid metals from which assays are made to determine the value of the bars. About thirty per cent of the value of the Comstock bullion bars is in gold, though it has at times run up to fifty per cent in some mines, and as low as ten per cent in others.

Though the Nevada Mill is in part driven by water, half the power used is electrically transmitted from six forty-inch Pelton water wheels set up in a large chamber excavated on the Sutro Tunnel level of the Chollar Mine, 1,630 feet below the surface. These small Pelton wheels drive six Brush dynamos, which generate the current that passes over the copper wires to the electric motors in the mill. The electric apparatus transmits to the main driving shaft of the mill about sixty-five per cent of the power developed by the Pelton wheels. Each Pelton wheel drives a dynamo, and one, two, four or all the dynamos may be run at the same time, just as may be required, each Pelton and dynamo being independent of the others.

After the water is used on the large-surface Pelton wheel in the mill it is caught up and by means of a small flume is conducted to the shaft of the Chollar Mine, near at hand, down which two large iron pipes carry it to the six small Peltons below. By thus twice using the same water a saving of one-half is made. The pressure on the lower Pelton wheels is immense. Never before has any water wheel been operated under a vertical pressure of 1,630 feet.

The Nevada Mill was built to work the ores of the Hale and Norcross, Chollar and Potosi Mines. It is one of the most substantial mills in the country, and no mill in the State is better arranged. It is lighted with electricity, and the grounds in front are illuminated by means of an arc light on a tall mast.

The Two California Mills.

The California stamp and pan-mills in Virginia City reduce the ores of the Consolidated California and Virginia Mine. The stamp-mill is situated immediately east of the C and C shaft of the mine. It contains eighty stamps. The ore crushed in this mill is amalgamated in the pan-mill, which stands about 1,500 feet further east. The crushed ore is conducted from the stamp-mill to the pan-mill through an iron pipe four inches in diameter. The process of amalgamation is much the same as at the Chollar Mill, except that the pulp goes directly into the amalgamating pans instead of being first received in settling tanks. It flows from pan to pan—the outflow of the first pan passing into the second through a pipe, thence into a third, and so on—and from settler to settler, being in all about three hours in passing through the series. This is called the Boss Continuous Process. It is in use in no other mill on the Comstock, as yet. In connection with the Rae electrical process of amalgamation (in which a current of electricity is passed through the settlers) it is found to work satisfactorily. The electric current prevents loss of "floured" quicksilver. Both mills are driven by Pelton water wheels. A single Pelton wheel eleven feet in diameter, placed on the surface, drives the eighty stamps of the battery-mill, and also twelve Boss grinding pans. The water used on the surface Pelton is caught up and conducted to the C and C shaft, where it is used on a series of Pelton wheels of the same size. These wheels are placed in chambers made for their reception 500 feet apart from the top of the shaft down to the Sutro Tunnel level (there 1,500 feet), and by means of steel wire cables, used as belts, the power of all the lower wheels is brought to a main driving shaft on the surface. The whole power is then transmitted to the pan-mill (about 1,600 feet) by means of steel wire cables passing over pulleys placed on a series of tall wooden towers. The cables pass over a considerable depression between the top of the C and C shaft and the pan-mill; three high towers are required in the middle portion.

River and Canyon Mills.

The Mexican Mill, on the Carson River, contains forty-four stamps and a corresponding number of pans, settlers, and other amalgamating machinery. The Morgan Mill has forty stamps. It works ore from the Consolidated California and Virginia Mine. The Brunswick Mill contains seventy-six stamps, the Vivian sixteen, Santiago thirty-eight, and Eureka sixty. All these mills are about and below Empire City, and all work Comstock ores. The Eureka Mill is run on ore from the Consolidated California and Virginia. The Rock Point Mill (thirty stamps), at Dayton, and the Douglas Mill (ten stamps), in Lower Gold Hill, also work Comstock ores.

At and about Silver City are two or three small

mills that work the ores of mines in that neighborhood, and on the Carson River are the Douglas and Woodworth Mills, which work tailings.

On Six-mile Canyon, below Virginia City to the east, are several small water mills having an aggregate of about thirty stamps. These work ores from the mines on the canyon and in Flowery District. On the canyon are also one or two small mills that work tailings and the concentrations from blanket sluices.

The Alta Mining Company has a ten-stamp mill, with concentrators, immediately adjoining the hoisting works at their mine. The Justice Company have a new ten-stamp mill near their mine.

Owing to the fact that many mines are now at the same time producing large quantities of ore, a lack of milling facilities is being felt. To meet this demand the Nevada Mill has been enlarged one-third, and the capacity of other mills will be increased, and perhaps some new mills will be erected. Processes by means of which low-grade ores may be profitably worked will no doubt yet be invented or discovered, which will cause many new works to be erected either on the Carson River or in the neighborhood of the mines producing large quantities of such ores.

THE COMSTOCK LODE.
Hoisting Works, Shafts, and Mining, Past and Present.

The Comstock Lode crops out along the eastern

face of Mount Davidson, about 1,200 feet below the summit, and just above the western suburbs of Virginia City. To the northward and southward the vein runs along the east side of other and smaller mountains of the same range. The face of Mount Davidson slopes to the east at an angle of about twenty-five degrees, and the vein dips in the same direction at an average inclination of forty-five degrees. It was at first supposed that the vein dipped to the west (into Mount Davidson), and the first hoisting works were erected on or near the croppings, where shafts were sunk and inclines sent down. For the first 400 to 500 feet the vein did pitch to the west into the mountain. Mount Davidson was then supposed to be the great central magazine, or nucleus, of all the silver found near the surface, and claims located on the slope of the mountain below to the eastward found but little favor in the eyes of mining men and would-be purchasers. Suddenly all this was changed, and there was a general "right-about-face." It was discovered in the Gould & Curry and the Ophir Mines that at a certain depth the lode became perpendicular, then turned and took a regular dip to the east, of about forty-five degrees, following as a footwall the syenite slope of Mount Davidson. It was then seen that the false dip above was caused by the top of the vein being bent over under the pressure of sliding material on the slope of the mountain at and near the surface.

THE THREE LINES OF HOISTING WORKS.

However, much ore was mined at the first line of works, particularly at the Ophir, Mexican, California, Gould & Curry, Savage, and Hale & Norcross Mines. But, as the dip of the vein was away from these first works, it presently became necessary to move to the eastward about 1,000 feet. As very deep shafts would there be required in order to intersect the lode, larger and much more powerful hoisting works and pumping machinery must be erected. Indeed, the new works required to be first-class in every respect, as the shafts would be far deeper than any yet put down on the lode, and it was by this time known that there would be immense quantities of water to handle.

Accordingly, the second line of fine and powerful first-class works, seen at present, and again in active use, was constructed. The shafts of the new line of works all cut into the heart of the vein, and in several the "bonanzas" found were so large and so rich as to astonish the whole mining world and create a much greater and far more widespread excitement than was seen when silver was first discovered in the croppings of the vein at the Ophir Mine. All the leading mines were soon taking out their tens of millions, but when the "big bonanza" was struck in the Consolidated Virginia and California the yield of gold and silver bullion soon became a matter of scores of millions. It was then that the fame of the Comstock

THE COMSTOCK LODE.

spread to every corner of the world, and the rush of speculators, fortune-seekers, and adventurers of all ages, sexes, and classes was greater than ever before. Though what is called the "Big Bonanza" was struck in the Consolidated Virginia in October, 1873, at a point on the 1,167-foot level, it was not until October, 1874, that the excitement in regard to it reached fever-heat. The main shaft had then reached the 1,500-foot level, and the ore disclosed by drifts and chambers was of such extraordinary and astonishing richness that experts could hardly believe their eyes or assayers their figures.

The Comstock Lode had a width (between the syenite wall on the west and the propylite on the east) of from 1,000 to 1,200 feet at the point where the "Big Bonanza" was struck. The space between the two walls was filled with what is locally termed "vein material" (gangue), and in this was found the ore body or "bonanza," which was in one place over 300 feet in width. This mass of ore yielded from $100 to $700 per ton, but in places were found masses of pure native silver and spots of ore so rich in black sulphuret and gold that to make assays of it was much like making assays of the pure metals. From the "Bonanza Mines" alone from 1873 up to 1882 were taken $111,975,761.39; but in 1879 the yield began to fall off as the vein was followed downward, and in 1882 the amount of bullion taken out was small, not paying expenses.

In the meantime (while the big bonanza of the Consolidated Virginia and California companies was being worked out) most of the leading companies had exhausted their second bonanzas. Instead of prospecting further in their immediate neighborhood, they all determined to go still farther east, sink a new line of shafts, and tap the vein at a still greater depth. This time they went out about 2,000 feet beyond their second line of hoisting works, or 3,000 feet east of the croppings of the lode. As it would be necessary to sink shafts to a depth of about 3,000 feet to intersect the vein, the hoisting works, hoisting machinery, and all else was made much larger, more powerful, and on a grander scale in every respect, than the second line. The principal works on this third line are those of the Combination shaft, New Yellow Jacket shaft, Osbiston and Union shafts, and the Forman shaft. In sinking these several companies united, the work was prosecuted with the greatest energy, and no expense was spared as regarded machinery and appliances.

THE COMBINATION SHAFT.

Of these shafts, that which attained the greatest vertical depth was the Combination—the joint shaft of the Chollar, Hale & Norcross, and Savage Companies. Before work on it was discontinued it had reached the great depth of 3,250 feet. There is but one deeper vertical shaft in the world. This is the

THE COMSTOCK LODE.

Adalbert Shaft, in the silver mines of Bohemia, which is 3,280 feet deep. There is no record of the time when work on this mine in Bohemia was commenced, though its written history extends back to 1527. The Combination Shaft was sunk at the rate of three feet a day, even in rock as hard as flint. The whole shaft is sunk in very hard rock (andesite), every foot of which had to be blasted. It is thirty feet by ten feet in size and is divided into four compartments for the accommodation of the hoisting and pumping apparatus.

The shaft was sunk to the depth of 2,200 feet before more water was encountered than could be hoisted out in the "skips" with the dirt. Down to the 2,400 level two Cornish pumps were used, each with columns fifteen inches in diameter. A drift run west into the vein tapped more water than the Cornish pumps could handle, when the management introduced hydraulic pumps. These pumps are run by the pressure of water from the surface through a pipe running down from the top of the shaft, whereas the Cornish pumps were run by huge steam engines. The shaft is connected with the Sutro drain tunnel at the depth of 1,600 feet, and to that point it was necessary to pump all the water. At the 3,000 level were placed a pair of hydraulic pumps, the deepest in the world. In Europe the deepest point at which a hydraulic pump has ever been worked is 2,700 feet. This is in the Hartz Mountains, in Germany.

When one stood at the 3,000 level and looked up a compartment of the shaft (five feet by six feet in size) the little spot of daylight seen at the top appeared to be about four inches square. At this great depth even the smallest bit of rock falling from the top whistles like a rifle-ball before reaching the bottom, and, striking a man on the head, would instantly kill him. Should a man fall that distance little would remain on which to hold an inquest—his body would be quite "dissipated." The Cornish and the hydraulic pumps working together had a daily capacity of 5,200,000 gallons—a small river! Hydraulic pumps were placed at the 2,400-foot level, the 2,600 and the 3,000 levels. Some idea of the great size of these engines and pumps may be formed when it is stated that the stations excavated for them were eighty-five feet long, twenty-eight feet wide, and twelve feet high. All this space was so filled with machinery that there was only room left to move about among it. Drifts were run to the west to the lode at the 2,400, 2,800 and 3,000-foot levels. On the 3,000 level the distance from the shaft to the east wall of the vein was found to be only 250 feet. The lode at this depth (3,000 feet) was found to be of great width and well mineralized—indeed the Hale & Norcross folks had a good showing of ore.

The Deepest Workings.

Although the Combination Shaft is the deepest vertical opening on the lode, it is not the point of deepest mining. The deepest workings are in the mine of the Union Consolidated Company, toward the north end of the lode. There long drifts were run and much prospecting done at the great depth of 3,350 feet. This depth was obtained by running a drift from the bottom of the vertical shaft and then sinking a winze from the drift.

The Yellow Jacket (new) shaft has a vertical depth of 3,050 feet, and much prospecting was done in the mine at a depth of 3,000 feet; also in the Belcher and Crown Point. In the Belcher excellent prospects were being obtained when the company were obliged to discontinue work. By connecting adjacent shafts by means of drifts and otherwise maintaining a proper system of ventilation miners experience no difficulty in working at any depth yet attained on the Comstock Lode.

A Return to the Second Line of Works.

February 13, 1882, a flow of water was tapped on the 2,700 level of the Exchequer Mine, that flooded not only that mine, but also the Alpha, Imperial, Yellow Jacket, Kentuck, Crown Point, Belcher, Overman, Segregated Belcher, and Caledonia. The water rushed to the Yellow Jacket Shaft, where the pumping was done which drained the advanced workings (most eastern) of all the mines named. The Yellow Jacket folks pumped and bailed an average flow of 110 miners inches a day for seven days. Though they were raising 1,320 gallons every minute the water gained on them and raised to the level (2,700) on which it was tapped by the Exchequer. The water had then filled all the drifts, cross-cuts, and winzes of the whole group of mines from the Bullion south to the Caledonia. Pumping was still continued, for the purpose of exhausting the subterranean reservoir in the Exchequer, till March 28, when the water had been so far reduced that there was a depth of only 950 feet above the 3,000 level of the Yellow Jacket Shaft. Then, as no combined arrangement could be made among the several companies interested to continue the work and drain all the mines, the Yellow Jacket Company stopped pumping and shut down their works. This stopped all work below the level of the Sutro drain tunnel, and the works have never since been started up. Had all the companies "stood in" for a time longer all the flooded mines would have been thoroughly drained.

The cost of the new works on the advanced line had been so much, and the expense incurred in hoisting and pumping from such great depths was so heavy, that stockholders in all the mines along the lode now became discouraged. They declared that what had happened in the case of the Gold Hill group of mines was liable to happen in the other deep workings, and began to clamor for a general return to the works at the second line of shafts, where it was known that pay ore had been left behind in the race after depth. When stockholders found that the deep shafts did not at once cut into pay ore, when they tapped the vein, they had no patience to wait for much prospecting to be done. They demanded that paying deposits be sought for at once in the old levels above the Sutro Tunnel, where there could be no trouble from water. Thus it happens that along the whole lode all the mining now being done is at the works situated over the second line of shafts, and above the level of the Sutro Tunnel. These shafts are by no means shallow, as they range in depth from 2,000 to 2,900 feet. The return has been fortunate. The vein being from 400 to 1,000 and even in places 1,400 feet in width between walls, it was very little explored in the neighborhood of the works of the second line of shafts. When the bonanzas in sight were exhausted, the universal cry was: "Get away to the east! Strike the lode at greater depths! Another 1,000 feet of depth will give us a third fertile zone—a third line of bonanzas!" Now it is being discovered that large and rich deposits of ore had been left behind—that they are scattered in all directions in the great breadth of vein material like plums in a pudding. Again dividends are the order of the day along the famous old lode.

The Old First Bonanzas.

Out of the first "bonanzas" great fortunes were taken. The bonanza of the Ophir, into which the first discoverers of silver—O'Riley and McLaughlin—accidentally dug, yielded about $20,000,000 before it was exhausted; the Savage, $16,500,000; Hale &

Norcross, $11,000,000; Chollar and Potosi, $16,000,000; Gould & Curry, $15,500,000; Yellow Jacket, $16,500,000; Crown Point, $22,000,000; Belcher, $26,000,000; Overman, $3,250,000; Imperial, $2,750,000, and the Kentuck, Sierra Nevada, Justice, and many other mines sums running from hundreds of thousands up into millions. In all, the yield of the mines on the Comstock Lode from the discovery down to the present time has been between $350,000,000 and $400,000,000. Of much of the silver and gold at first taken from the lode, both at Gold Hill and Virginia City, there is no record; and in many instances since that time much gold and silver bullion has been obtained from ores, tailings, slimes, and sulphurets that was never fully accounted for.

The New Departure.

In the new departure, of which a return to the second line of hoisting works was the leading feature, the two bonanza mines—the California and the Consolidated Virginia—were consolidated and incorporated as one mine under the name of the Consolidated California and Virginia. Work was resumed in the old upper levels and soon small streaks of low-grade ore, that had formerly been passed by, led to deposits of fair milling ore. In working these deposits other bodies were found, and finally many new and valuable ore bodies were developed. A fire which had been smouldering for about ten years in a section of the old workings was extinguished by the use of carbonic acid gas, and this gave access to large deposits of milling ore that had not before been available. This and the new discoveries soon gave the company large bodies of ore in a number of places above the Sutro Tunnel level. Again many miners were employed, and the output of ore became sufficient to keep many stamps in constant operation.

The total yield of the " Big Bonanza," in the California and Consolidated Virginia, was as follows: Consolidated Virginia, $65,116,822.69; California, $46,858,938.70, making a total of $111,975,761.39. Out of this the Consolidated Virginia paid dividends amounting to $42,930,000, and the California a total of $31,320,000 in dividends.

Present Yield of Leading Mines.

Since the consolidation of the two mines, the Consolidated California and Virginia has yielded $8,001,856.95, and has paid dividends amounting to $2,440,800, up to and including December, 1888. The total yield of the great ore deposit known as the " Big Bonanza," from the time of its discovery to the end of December, 1888 (under both incorporations), was $119,977,618.34, and the total amount of dividends to the same date was $76,690,800. To give an idea of the rate of the present yield of the mine the following details are furnished: For the quarter that ended March 31, 1888, the mine produced 39,552 tons of ore, yielding $921,903.77 in bullion, an average of

$23 30 a ton. In April (1888) there was worked a total of 13,893 tons of ore, yielding bullion to the value of $418,729.43. The average assay value a ton was 36.83, and the average yield a ton was $30.13. In May the yield was $411,173.13; in June, $405,834.08; July, $206,672.26; August, $352,554.97; September, $267,386.18; October, $339,814.45; November, $220,373.74; and in December, $260,320.56. The falling off in the month of July and thereafter throughout the year was due to the dry season in the summer and a phenomenally dry fall and winter. In January, 1889, there was a fair milling stage of water in the Carson River the greater part of the time, and the yield of bullion rose to $267,847.51.

The mine has kept the Morgan and Eureka Mills going to their full capacity whenever there was sufficient water to run them at all. Owing to a scarcity of water at the sources of supply in the Sierra Nevada Mountains, the Virginia and Gold Hill Water Company have for some months been unable to furnish water for the two California Mills in this city; to furnish water to the Nevada Mill has been a heavy draft on the reservoirs. With proper storage reservoirs in the Sierras the mills on the Carson River might be run the year round. At present eighty per cent of all the water flows into the "sinks" and is lost.

More mines on the Comstock are at the present time producing paying ore than ever before in the history of the lode. The following mines are now ore producing: Consolidated California and Virginia, Gould & Curry, Occidental, Ophir, Andes, Savage, Hale & Norcross, Chollar, Potosi, Confidence, Challenge, Yellow Jacket, Belcher, Crown Point, Alta, Justice, Overman, Baltimore, and Kentuck. Several other companies who own mines on the lode have quartz that yields promising assays in the precious metals, and are liable at any time to find paying deposits.

To show the rate at which some of the mines have been paying during the past year, though handicapped by an unusually dry season and a lack of milling facilities, I give a few statistics, as follows: During the quarter that ended March 31, 1888, the Chollar Company milled 1,415 tons of ore that yielded $21,795.70 in bullion; the Confidence 1,722 tons, yielding $42,541.72; Hale & Norcross, 7,958 tons, yielding $236,047.32; Kentuck, 1,027 tons, yielding $13,055.50; Potosi, 3,050 tons, yielding $56,461.16, and the Yellow Jacket, 16,780 tons, yielding $121,027.82.

For the quarter ending June 30, 1888, the Hale & Norcross yielded 18,075 tons of ore, that produced $451,740 in bullion; the Chollar, 4,750 tons, yielding $74,507; Confidence, 17,285 tons, yielding $401,293; Yellow Jacket, 7,080 tons, yielding $55,022.

For the quarter that ended September 30, the Hale & Norcross yielded 6,365 tons of ore, that produced $173,941.80 in bullion; Confidence, 9,207 tons, yielding $176,064.93; Yellow Jacket, 1,370 tons, yielding $9,932.

For the quarter that ended December 30, 1888, the Chollar milled 2,835 tons that yielded $38,130.81: Challenge, 1,875 tons, yielding $31,096.16; Confidence, 6,195 tons, yielding $105,970.59; Yellow Jacket, 3,388 tons, yielding $25,856; Savage, 5,292 tons, yielding $66,422.75; Hale & Norcross, 4,820 tons, yielding $90,015.59, and the Alta, 946 tons, yielding $23,330.

The Consolidated California and Virginia has steadily paid $108,000 monthly in dividends. The Confidence and Hale & Norcross also paid dividends during 1888 at the rate of from $49,000 to $50,000 a month. And during the year the pay rolls of the several companies have aggregated from $250,000 to over $300,000 a month.

During 1888, new bodies of ore were found in the Consolidated California and Virginia, Hale & Norcross, Confidence, Yellow Jacket, Crown Point, Gould & Curry, Savage, Chollar, Potosi, Best & Belcher, and some others. Crown Point and Belcher have made connection with the Sutro drain tunnel, and are again working below that level. Eventually the leading companies will get back into the deep workings now deserted.

Vicissitudes of Fortune in Mining.

The vicissitudes of fortune are probably more striking in mining for silver than in any other kind of mining. In all silver-producing countries we are told of mines being again and again abandoned because it was thought their rich "bonanzas" had been exhausted, but they have again and again been reopened and new and rich bodies of ore discovered. The Valenciana Mine, on the Veta Macbee (mother vein), of Guanaguato, Mexico, was reopened in 1760, on a part of the vein where work had been done in the sixteenth century, and which had afterwards lain as worthless for 200 years, and in 1768 a bonanza was struck at a depth of only 240 feet, from which $1,500,000 was extracted annually. And from 1788 to 1810 the annual average was still $1,383,195. At a depth of 1,200 feet the ore was considered too poor for extracting, and the mine was allowed to fill with water. Afterwards it was again opened and again paid immensely by working the almost inexhaustible quantities of low-grade ore.

The Veta Grande, at Zacatecas, which from 1548 to 1832 yielded $660,000,000, occurs in propalite, as does the Comstock, and has a similar structure, the vein branching out toward the surface, and dipping at an angle of forty-five degrees. It is, however, much smaller than the Comstock. It averages only about thirty-three feet, and eighty feet is its greatest width. In the upper part the ore was found concentrated in chimneys, but at depth it was found to be distributed through nearly the whole width of the vein. At first this low grade material could not be made to pay, but since it has been profitably worked and the bullion product has reached a high figure. Scores of such examples may be found in all silver-producing countries, as chronicled by Humboldt, Ward, Von Cotta, and others.

Even when no more large deposits of rich ore are to be found on the Comstock, there are immense and almost inexhaustible areas of low-grade ore upon which to fall back. In working these small bonanzas are sure to be encountered—scattered plums in the pudding—which will assist in sending up the average. New processes for working and concentrating ores are constantly being discovered, new methods in mining are being introduced, and new labor-saving machinery is almost daily being invented. Waterpower, steam, compressed air, and electricity are fast taking the place of muscle. Each year machinery guided by mind is lessening the work to be done by mere power of muscle. Already the cost of milling has been greatly reduced, as has the cost of transporting ores and the cost of wood, lumber, and mining timbers. Present expenses will shortly be still further reduced.

TOWNS OF WESTERN NEVADA.

Virginia City having been sufficiently well described in connection with the Comstock Lode, it now remains to briefly mention the other towns of Western Nevada. These all lie near the Sierras within a space of ter-

Gold Hill.

ritory forty-four miles long and twenty-five miles wide—under the "eaves" of the mountains.

Gold Hill.

The town of Gold Hill was originally about one mile south of Virginia City—a mile south of where silver was first struck in the Ophir Mine. Buildings now unite the two towns. The boundary line between the two places is on the ridge called the "Divide," but at that point there is no break in the rows of buildings on the streets. Gold Hill is built along the deep and narrow gorge that forms the head of Gold Canyon. From the north line on the Divide it straggles down the hill and along down the canyon for a distance of about two miles—almost down to Silver City indeed, the main business street following what was formerly the channel of the ravine.

There were houses and settlers in Gold Hill before there were either in Virginia City, therefore it is the older town. Here it was that the Comstock Lode was first struck—though not the silver ore—by "Old Virginia" (John Bishop) and others, who were prospecting for placer mines. The town is 6,000 feet above the level of the sea, and, being shut in on the east and west sides by hills, it is always two or three degrees warmer than Virginia, 1,000 feet above on the mountain-side.

The first miners at Gold Hill were really at work in a "chimney" of the Comstock, a little hill sometimes called "Gold Hill proper," to distinguish the hill from

the town. Much gold was taken out of the top of this chimney, and at depth it yielded many millions in silver. Although scores of millions have been taken out of the vein beneath the foundations of the town, it is still yielding its millions, and still new ore bodies are being developed in the great vein.

Under the town are situated the world-famous Crown Point, Belcher, Yellow Jacket, Imperial, Kentuck, Confidence, and other mines, while farther down the canyon (under Lower Gold Hill) are the Overman, Alta, Benton, Justice, and several other well-known mines. The mining works in the town are in every respect first-class and are lighted with electric lamps. In the town are many fine buildings, both public and private. There is a handsome Catholic Church, and the High School building is one of the best buildings of the kind in the State. The Miners' Union have a commodious hall on Main Street, and the other societies and orders have fine halls. Conspicuous among the private residences of the town is that of U. S. Senator J. P. Jones—the "Jones mansion," as it is familiarly called. The town has an abundant supply of water (from the Virginia and Gold Hill Water Company's works), and is well supplied with fire hydrants; it also has electrical lights. In 1878 the population was about 8,000, but it is now less than half that number. About the town are many handsome private grounds. Shade and ornamental trees begin to abound, and to the north, towering hundreds of feet above the town, are picturesque castellated piles of bare granite rocks. The Virginia and Truckee Railroad passes through the town.

Silver City.

Silver City is situated on Gold Canyon, a short distance below Lower Gold Hill. The two towns are separated by a rugged ridge of porphyritic rock, through which is a pass only three or four rods wide, known as the Devil's Gate. About and below Silver City much gravel mining was done by the Johntowners in the early days. It was at Silver City that the first silver mill (Paul's Pioneer) was built. It had a newspaper—the *Washoe Times*—before a newspaper was published in Virginia, the *Territorial Enterprise* being then (1860) published in Carson City. At one time it had many big silver mills and promised to be the big town of the State; but the tide turned and all crowded in about the big mines at Virginia City. The town contains at present a population of only about 600. There is a fine public-school building, church, Miners' Union Hall, and many handsome and comfortable dwellings, with an adequate supply of saloons, stores, and shops.

About the town are an immense number of small veins of gold-bearing quartz that pay from the surface down. Nearly every head of a family in the town has his own mine, and when he wants money he shoulders his pick, goes out to his mine, and digs it, as a farmer in the East digs a "mess" of potatoes. Of late some large veins have been opened up in and about the town—as the Oest, Hawood, and others—and Silver City bids fair soon to become a busy mining center. The people have lived off their home mines for thirty years, and constitute the most thoroughly independent mining community to be found in Nevada.

Dayton.

Dayton, the county seat of Lyon County, lies five miles below Silver City, on the Carson River, at the mouth of Gold Canyon. The beginning of this town was a log building, erected as a dwelling and trading-post by John McMarlin, in the fall of 1849. Being on the overland wagon road passing over the Sierras by the Placerville route, there was a good deal of trade with incoming immigrants, as well as with the miners, who soon began to earn from $8.00 to $12 a day in the gravel bank and bars of Gold Canyon. In 1856, about fifty Chinamen came over the mountains and began mining on the lower part of the canyon, working over the banks and bars left by the white miners. In 1858, nearly 200 Chinamen were at work in the canyon from its mouth up toward Johntown. These had their shanties about McMarlin's store, and the place took the name of "Chinatown," by which name it was known at the time of the discovery of silver.

In 1861 an attempt was made (many whites having then settled there) to give the place the name of "Nevada City." This did not take, as there was already a Nevada City in California, and for a time the town was called "Mineral Rapids," but this finally gave way to the present name of Dayton. The place grew apace, it being then expected that nearly all the ore of the Comstock would be worked at and near the town in mills driven by water-power. This hope was not realized, though several fine mills were built near the town. It had in 1878 a population of about 1,200, and has since held its own very well. Though not a very large town, it has always been a very pleasant and flourishing one.

The Carson and Colorado Railroad passes through the town, and from this a branch built in 1888 extends down the river to the Rock Point Mill. Here (at Dayton) is to be the scene of the operations of the Carson River Dredging Company, an Eastern incorporation headed by Dr. J. H. Rae. The object is to pump up from the bottom of the Carson River the millions in gold and silver, amalgam, and quicksilver, washed into the river and lost with the tailings running from the many mills. No doubt the "millions" found their way into the river, but whether they can be brought out of its bottom by means of a big suction pump remains to be seen. It is the universal wish that the dredger may prove a success. All will be in readiness to try it this season on a large scale.

Dayton contains good public buildings of all kinds required, both county and town, has several mills, and many handsome private residences, surrounded with gardens and fruit and shade trees. In summer the place is completely embowered.

The acid works of J. M. Douglass & Co. manufacture daily two tons of sulphuric acid. The sulphur used is a native product of Nevada, and is brought from the mine in Humboldt County at a cost of $40 a ton. Dayton is surrounded with a fine agricultural and grazing region. A narrow-gauge railroad five miles long runs down the river from the Douglass Mill to a large tailings reservoir.

Sutro.

Sutro is a town laid off at the mouth of the Sutro Tunnel by Adolph Sutro. Mr. Sutro claimed that his town would kill Virginia City, as all the reduction works would be located there, and all the miners would reside there, passing to and from their work through the tunnel. As there would no longer be any need of anyone remaining in Virginia, the place would be given up to bats and owls—coyotes would sit upon the peak of Mount Davidson and "bay the moon." Believing Mr. Sutro to have got hold of the mantle of some ancient financial prophet, many persons were induced to flee the "wrath to come" (bats, owls and coyotes), and settle down at the mouth of the tunnel. There was quite a brisk little town there for a few years, but when the tunnel was completed and the miners discharged Sutro's " bats and owls " came home to roost—they found no rest for the soles of their feet at Virginia. Once the men who had been engaged in driving the tunnel went away, there was nothing more to make or keep up a town than at any other point along the edge of the valley; for the big reduction works promised by Mr. Sutro were never built.

Carson City.

Carson City is the county seat of Ormsby County and the capital of Nevada. It is situated in Eagle Valley, immediately east of the high-timbered hills forming the eastern base of the main range of the Sierra Nevada Mountains. Unlike the majority of Nevada towns, it has a dry, level plain for its site. The city was laid out in 1858 by Major Ormsby and others. The streets conform to the cardinal points of the compass. There being no lack of level land, the streets were made sixty-six and eighty feet wide. Previous to 1858 there was no town where Carson now stands, and only one house, which was at Eagle Ranch, which ranch gave its name to the valley in which it was situated. Afterwards this ranch became better known as King's Ranch.

Carson City grew rapidly from the start, for it was not only pleasantly situated, but also occupied an advantageous position as a center of trade. For several years in its infancy it derived a good deal of benefit from its trade with the great immigrant trains that yearly rattled in across the "plains;" besides, it was a halting-place for people rushing to the silver mines from the California side of the mountains. In nearly all directions it is surrounded by excellent agricultural and grazing lands. With the regular and scientific opening of the mines Carson became the headquarters of an enormous trade in wood, lumber, and mining timbers, a business it still retains. The city has at present a population of about 4,100.

Carson contains many fine and costly buildings, both public and private. The pride of the city is the State Capitol. It is the most striking structure in the place. The building is handsome architecturally, being well proportioned in all its parts. It also has a very substantial appearance, as it is constructed of stone throughout. This stone is a beautiful, fine-grained sandstone obtained from a quarry at the State prison, about a mile and a half east of the town. The building was erected in 1870. The Capitol occupies the center of a square several acres in extent. This square is surrounded with a handsome and substantial iron fence. The grounds are handsomely laid out and well kept. They are well swarded and contain a great variety of shade and ornamental trees, shrubbery, and flowering plants. The whole is a credit to the State.

The U. S. Branch Mint building is a large, substantial, and imposing structure. It is also of stone, from the State Prison quarry. The building was completed in July, 1869. It has done and is still doing a great deal of work.

The State Orphans' Home is a large and well-arranged building with a small farm in connection therewith. In this institution a great number of orphan children from all sections of the State are cared for. The home is governed in a paternal way, and the children are well clothed, well fed, and well educated both morally and intellectually.

The town contains several churches of leading denominations, excellent school-houses, and a number of halls of various societies, orders, and lodges. There are half a dozen fine hotels, many large fire-proof stores and business houses, with the usual proportion of neat and attractive retail shops of all kinds, saloons, and the like.

The buildings of the Virginia and Truckee Railroad Company are a noticeable feature of the town. The depot buildings are commodious and conveniently arranged, and are always kept neatly painted and in good repair. In the town they have an immense car shop. The building is in large part constructed of iron. In it are a foundry, machine shop, roundhouse, and car manufactory.

Carson has a large box factory and other manufacturing establishments of several kinds. The place has both electrical lights and gas. It is well supplied with pure mountain water, which is led through all the streets under a heavy pressure. The town site has sufficient slope to the eastward to afford good drainage. The city supports two daily newspapers, the *Appeal* and *Tribune*, and has a good theater.

A fine large brick building has this year (1889) been erected in the town by the United States Government. It will contain several public offices. It fills a gap in the center of the town that long stood as a staring vacancy—supplies a "long-felt want."

There are pleasant drives in all directions from Carson, with smooth and level roads. A mile west of town are Shaw's Hot Springs, with every convenience for either bathing or swimming. The swimming bath is 60 by 24 feet, 4½ feet deep at one end and 5½ at the other.

All visitors to the town of a scientific turn of mind will wish to visit the State prison and grounds, situated a mile and a half east of the place. A portion of the building now occupied as a State prison was built for a hotel by Col. Abe Curry (of whom the State purchased the property), and was of stone, two stories high, 32 feet wide, and 100 feet long. Colonel Curry also excavated and walled up the magnificent swimming bath now connected with the prison and fed by warm springs.

In the floor of the quarry, beneath from fifteen to twenty feet of strata of sandstone, is a stratum of fine-grained stone that is filled with the tracks of all manner of animals and birds, and even one set of tracks supposed to have been made by some prehistoric giant of the human species. There are tracks of elephants, horses, deer, lions, tigers, panthers, giant cranes, and all manner of creatures. The tracks supposed to be human present the appearance of having been made by a large man wearing moccasins of the undressed hide of some animal. All the tracks tend toward a common point, which must have been a spring or small lake.

Omnibuses run to the Hot Springs and the State prison, and stages leave for Lake Tahoe and Genoa on the arrival of trains.

There are several lumber flumes near Carson that are worthy of inspection.

Empire City.

This town is situated on the banks of the Carson River, three and a half miles east of Carson, and on the line of the Virginia and Truckee Railroad. Empire is pre-eminently a milling town. Here are located the Mexican, Morgan, Brunswick, and Merrimac Mills, all first-class silver reduction works. The town is in Ormsby County, and contains about 700 inhabitants. Each year thousands of cords of wood floated down the Carson River from Alpine County, California, are taken out here. Formerly no fewer than 150,000 cords of wood came down to this town in the drives of a single season. On account of these wood drives Empire was jockularly termed the "seaport" of Nevada. The wood "drives" and the landing of them for a time each year gave employment to a great number of men and teams.

The town contains a number of handsome residences and a few good public buildings.

Genoa.

Genoa is the oldest town in Nevada, and is the place where the first white settlement was made. These settlers were Mormons, and they established a station there as early as 1848. For this reason the place was long known as "Mormon Station." For several years most of the settlers in the valley and about the town were Mormons. Genoa is the county seat of Douglas County, and is situated in Carson Valley, at a point about 13 miles south of Carson City. Although in a beautiful valley it lies close in against the Sierras, at an altitude of 4,335 feet above the level of the sea. To the westward the main timbered Sierra Nevada Mountain Range rises to a great height, while above its ridge tower many bald, granite peaks. Among these (to the southward) Job's Peak rises to the height of 10,639 feet.

The town contains a fine court-house, and other handsome public buildings, as school-houses, churches, and halls. There are in the place several good, substantial stores, and business houses and shops. There are many neat dwellings and cottages surrounded with fine gardens and grounds. In the town is published the Genoa *Courier*, a sprightly weekly paper devoted to the interests of the people of the town and county. In this town was first published (in 1859) the *Territorial Enterprise*, the pioneer newspaper of Nevada. The paper was moved to Carson in 1860, and thence in a short time to Virginia City, where it was soon made a daily, and where it has ever since been published as such.

Fine ranches lie up and down the valley. A mile and a half south of the town are Walley's famous hot springs, of which more particular mention will be found in another place. Lake Tahoe forms part of the western boundary of Douglas, and both Glenbrook and Cave Rock are in the county. The Carson River passes near Genoa and through the heart of the county. Genoa contains about 1,000 inhabitants.

Reno.

Reno, on the line of the Central Pacific Railroad, and pleasantly situated on the banks of the beautiful Truckee River, is the county seat of Washoe County. Reno began to be a town in 1868, and under the influence of the Central Pacific Railroad, it grew very rapidly. The town at once became the shipping-point of all goods, machinery, and supplies destined for the Comstock Mines, and for all parts of Storey, Lyon, Ormsby, and Douglas Counties; also for Susanville, Honey Lake Valley, and a great scope of country to the northward. In the days before the completion of the Virginia and Truckee Railroad, Reno was filled with teams and stage coaches. The place was a sort of teamsters' paradise. This was good for the town, but it could not be expected to last forever. The present ambition of the place is to become a railroad and manufacturing center. It has the Virginia and Truckee Road leading southward, while to the northward the Nevada and California is fast advancing to completion.

Reno is the center of one of the finest agricultural and grazing sections in the State, and is a point for the shipment to California of immense numbers of beef cattle. Although there are in the town large and fine reduction works for smelting refractory ores, and two flouring mills, it may be said that hardly a commencement has been made toward the utilization of the immense water-power afforded by the Truckee River at and near the town.

Here is located the Nevada Insane Asylum, the building and grounds of which do credit to the town and State. The State University is also now located at Reno (having been removed from Elko), and is in a more flourishing condition than ever before. The buildings, and grounds, and teachers are all that could be desired. This institution has recently been made an Agricultural Experiment Station. Here is located Bishop Whitakers' excellent school for young ladies, and also a similar school, first-class, in charge of the Sisters of Charity. There are, besides, five public schools. The town is well supplied with churches and public buildings of all kinds adequate to present requirements.

The town contains many first-class fire-proof business houses, five depots and railroad buildings, many attractive retail stores and shops, excellent and commodious hotels, "palatial" saloons, and handsome and comfortable private residences. It is lighted with electrical lamps, has good water works, and almost everything else that its public-spirited citizens have thought it necessary to provide. It has two excellent daily newspapers, the *Gazette* and *Journal*, and a first-class theater. This spring (1889) there has been in the place a boom in town property, and much building is in progress. Not only is the town on the highway of the nations of the world leading East and West, but is on the highway of the Pacific Coast leading North and South, along the great range of the Sierra Nevada Mountains, from Oregon to Arizona. The present population is estimated at 5,000 souls.

OTHER TOWNS IN WASHOE COUNTY.

It may be worth while for the satisfaction of persons traveling southward from Reno on the Virginia and Truckee, to mention some once promising towns in Washoe County that now only exist as sleepy hamlets:—

WASHOE CITY.—This place is situated at the North end of Washoe Valley, sixteen miles south of Reno. It was formerly the county seat of Washoe County, and contained about seven hundred inhabitants. There was in the town a substantial brick courthouse, Masonic and Odd Fellows' Hall, Methodist Church, public school building, good hotels, and many stores, shops, and saloons.

OPHIR.—This town, three miles south of Washoe City, on the west side of Washoe Lake, at one time contained two or three hundred inhabitants. Here was situated a big seventy-stamp mill erected by the Ophir Mining Company at a cost of over $500,000. To reach this mill with ores from the Ophir Mine a bridge a mile in length was built across the north end of Washoe Lake, at a cost of $75,000. The ores were amalgamated by the barrel or Freyburg process, and everything was on a grand scale, the buildings covering over an acre of ground.

FRANKTOWN.—This town, one mile south of Ophir, was originally settled by Mormons (about the same time of the settlement at Genoa). Mormon fashion, it was laid off in four-acre lots, and small streams of water ran through all the streets. Here John Dall had a thirty-stamp water mill, and there were several other mills on Franktown Creek. The town had over two hundred inhabitants in 1869.

At one time there were in operation in Washoe County ten mills (four or five near Washoe City), having an aggregate of 281 stamps, but the completion of the Virginia and Truckee Railroad to the Carson River was sudden death to all the mills, and killed all the towns. All the ore went to the river.

WADSWORTH, on the Central Pacific, thirty-four miles east of Reno, is a bright and growing little town. It is situated at the "Big Bend" of the Truckee River, a place well known to those who toiled across the plains in the early days. The place contains about 600 inhabitants. In it are the machine shops, round-house, and freight depot of the Central Pacific, and many good and substantial buildings, both public and private. Before the Carson and Colorado Railroad was built, Wadsworth was a shipping-point for many mining towns and camps to the southward. It still has a very fair trade.

VERDI, eleven miles west of Reno, on the Central Pacific, is a pleasant little lumbering town on the Truckee River, at the eastern base of the Sierras. It is a town of saw-mills and of manufactories of articles made of wood. In the way of mills and machinery Verdi contains a large amount of valuable property.

LAKE TAHOE.
Surrounding Objects of Interest.

All visitors to the Pacific Coast who are lovers of the beautiful and picturesque in natural scenery, will endeavor to spend some time at Lake Tahoe. Taking into consideration the surroundings, there is nowhere in the world a more grandly beautiful mountain lake. The lake lies between the eastern and western summit ridges of the main ridge of the Sierra Nevada Mountains, at an elevation of 6,247 feet above the level of the sea. Its length is a little over twenty-one miles, and its width about twelve miles. Roughly it has the form of a parallelogram, lying nearly north and south, about one-third in Nevada and the remainder in California. It has an area of 204 square miles, as is shown by measurements made in four places across its width, and longitudinally (north and south) in three places. Its greatest depth is 1,800 feet.

It is shut in and surrounded on all sides by mountains that rise to a height of from 2,000 to 5,000 feet above its surface. The lake evidently occupies an extinct volcanic crater of great size. Soundings show in the bottom a deep channel or crevice which extends nearly the whole length of the lake in a north and south direction. In this the depth is everywhere from 1,500 to 1,700 feet. The deepest spot (1,800 feet) is toward the south end of the lake, in front of Mount Tallac. The water is of great purity and crystal clearness, and never freezes.

The lake receives the waters of fifty-one creeks and brooks, the largest of which is the Upper Truckee, which falls in at the south end. It also receives the aqueous contributions of almost innumerable ravines, gorges, and canyons. It drains an area of over 500 square miles, composed largely of lofty mountains on which the snow falls to a depth of many feet, and by the melting of which the numerous streams are fed. There are also many living springs on the sides of the surrounding mountains, with a great number (both hot and cold) along the shores of the lake, and doubtless a much larger number deep beneath its surface. The only outlet of the lake is the Truckee

River, at its northwest corner. This outlet, which forms the head of the Truckee River, is fifty feet in width, has an average depth of five feet, and a velocity of six feet a second, making the discharge 123,120,000 cubic feet in twenty-four hours, in early spring when the snow in the mountains is rapidly melting.

Since it was first seen by white men the lake has been given several different names. Tahoe is popularly supposed to be a Washoe Indian word, that means "big water." Some say the word means "deep water," "clear water," "elevated water," or "bright water." The Washoe Indians themselves say they know nothing about the word. Fremont saw it in 1844, and simply called it "Mountain Lake." It was once mapped as "Lake Bonpland," and in 1859 was mapped by Dr. Henry De Groot as "Lake De Groot." It was also once known as "Lake Bigler," being so named by some in honor of a Democratic Governor of California, and the name is still used by some of the strait-laced among the Democracy. Tahoe, whatever it may mean, is a name now so universally acknowledged and so firmly fixed that it is not likely that it will ever be supplanted by any other.

Lake Tahoe is surrounded on all sides by mountains that have an elevation of from 3,000 to 5,000 feet above its surface. Mount Tallac towers to a height of 11,000 feet above the level of the sea; Pyramid Peak, 10,000; Monument Peak, 10,090;

Rubicon Peaks, fifteen miles west of the lake, 9,284; Job's Peak, 10,637; Sand Mountain, back of Rowland's, 8,747 feet; and Bald Mountain, Mount Pluto, Mount Anderson, Old Hat, Mount Ellis, Barker's Peak, Table Mountain, the Cliffs, the Needles, and many other peaks, rise to a height of over 8,000 feet. On all sides great old peaks stand about gazing down forever upon their reflected images in the lake below. It is a grand convocation of mountains, a convention of granite peaks, gray and ancient. In a circle about the lake stand pine-clad mountains, snow-clad mountains, and unclad mountains that are merely stupendous piles of granite—granite cathedrals piled up by nature for the delectation of those of her votaries that ever gladly worship at her shrine.

In places towering rocks stand quite near the water, and around the shores are so many bays and inlets, so many jutting points and tongues of land, that there is a constant change of views—an endless succession of either grand or picturesque effects. A single cliff—as Shakespeare Rock—seen from different points and distances, takes a dozen different shapes, and so of all prominent capes and caves. The distance round the shores of the lake is 144 miles, and may be said to represent that many miles of landscape panorama of unrivaled beauty and grandeur. Volumes have already been written descriptive of the wonders and the beauties of Lake Tahoe, and innumerable volumes will still be written as the ages pass, yet to comprehend the place it must be seen and *felt.*

It speaks well for Lake Tahoe that its beauties are appreciated and prized by persons living near by in California and Nevada, and that it is a favorite place of summer resort with the people everywhere on the Pacific Coast. In the Bible it is said: "A prophet is not without honor, save in his own country and in his own house," and the same may generally be said of celebrated natural objects, but it is different in the case of Tahoe—the grand and picturesque scenery of the lake is admired and esteemed at home. It is not only looked upon as being a great sanitarium of the Pacific Coast, but also as a grand store-house of all the delights of mountain scenery. In Tahoe the careworn and debilitated find a cure for both mind and body.

The water of the lake is as cold and pure as that of the best living springs, and it possesses wonderful charms—almost the transparency of the atmosphere. Near the shore, when shallow, it is of an emerald green here; in deep water, in the sunshine, it is of an ultramarine tinge, and in the shade an indigo blue. Tossing, distant, deep water in certain lights assumes tints of purple and violet, with beautiful flashes of ruby. Seated in a boat on the lake in a calm, one may see the stones and pebbles at the bottom, with trout cruising about, where the sounding line shows seventy-five feet of water. The whole dome of the sky, with every fleecy cloud, is there perfectly reflected.

We are midway between the heavens above and the heavens below, gently rocking upon the waving veil of blue that separates the two firmaments.

It is difficult to swim in the lake. Some have supposed this to be on account of the great elevation and reduced atmospheric pressure on the water, rendering the lake less buoyant than bodies of fresh water at sea level. This, however, is a mistake. Water is only very slightly compressible. The great purity of the water of course renders it less dense than that of lakes holding minerals in solution, but it is the coldness of the water and the variety of the atmosphere that render swimming difficult and laborious.

The bodies of persons drowned in the lake (unless very near shore) are never again seen. The bodies of no fewer than ten or twelve white men are known to lie at the bottom of the lake; and no doubt among them lie the skeletons of not a few Indians. The lake is in some respects treacherous and dangerous. It is subject to sudden and heavy squalls. Fierce gusts of wind at times rush down the big canyons, and, striking the water, cause it to boil like a pot. These squalls are liable to capsize a sail-boat. Unless an experienced boatman be of the party, it is best to have the sail in hand, that it may be let go in a moment. The squalls generally plunge down the canyons and gorges on the west side of the lake.

The route of the passenger steamers round the lake is near the shores. These are in some places rocky and in others level. In the mountain gorges and on the ridges are pines and various other evergreen trees, but down near the edge of the water are small groves of quaking asp, willow, and other trees of deciduous foliage.

At the Hot Springs is a good hotel, bathing houses, and other accommodations. At Tahoe City will also be found good hotels, boats, fishing tackle, and all such little sporting supplies as the visitor is likely to require. McKinney's, at Sugar Pine Point, on the west side of the lake, is a popular place of resort and possesses many attractions. At Glenbrook, on the east side of the lake, are good hotel accommodations, and there may also be had boats, fishing tackle, and all ordinary supplies. In many charming nooks and valleys around the shores are hotels and cottages for the accommodation of visitors.

EMERALD BAY.—One of the most beautiful spots about Lake Tahoe is Emerald Bay. It is the gem of the place. The bay is situated at the south end of the lake. It is 2½ miles long and 1¼ wide, nearly as large as Donner Lake. The entrance to it is through a channel less than 200 yards in width, but containing a depth of water sufficient to float a man-of-war. Emerald Bay is surrounded by grand and picturesque mountains, the peaks of which are 9,000 feet above the level of the sea, and some of which rise precipitously to a height of 4,000 feet above the surface of the bay. The water is nearly always of a beautiful emerald green. In the bay is a rocky and romantic little island of about three acres, on which is a handsome little cottage. On the island is a tomb excavated in the rock by an old boatman known as "Captain Dick." Captain Dick fondly hoped that this tomb would be his last resting-place, but his body lies at the bottom of the lake. In October, 1873, his boat was capsized in a furious squall, and Captain Dick was never seen again.

Emerald Bay, with 519 acres of surrounding land, belongs to the estate of the late Dr. P. T. Kirby, of Virginia City, who at the time of his death was about to build a fine and commodious hotel. Before his death, however, he had built over a dozen neat cottages. Heretofore, owing to lack of accommodations there, many tourists have failed to visit this bay, the most beautiful nook about the lake, but it will now at once become a favorite haunt of all lovers of the grand, picturesque, and beautiful. The island is a little gem, and has about it a style that gives it almost the appearance of being a toy constructed by a landscape gardener. It has been very appropriately named "Coquette Island." It rises to a height of about 200 feet above the surface of the bay. At the south end of the bay are the "Lovers' Falls." These falls are high up on the side of a steep and rocky mountain. They are on a small creek which makes many leaps down perpendicular terraces of rock. The falls are supposed to have been the favorite tryst of a Digger chief and his Washoe lady-love.

FALLEN LEAF LAKE.—This lake lies one mile south of Lake Tahoe, and about three miles south of Emerald Bay. It is a beautiful sheet of water two miles in length and a mile in width. It has an outlet into Lake Tahoe.

SILVER LAKE.—Silver Lake is a perfect little beauty in its way, but is seldom visited, as it lies high on the side of a mountain which is covered with chaparral. It is about half as large as Fallen Leaf Lake, from which it is distant two miles in a northwest direction.

CORNELIAN BAY.—This bay lies north of Tahoe City, and has a smooth, pebbly beach, where are found agates, cornelians, and jasper of several colors. To sail along the shore the distance from Tahoe City is seven miles.

AGATE BAY.— Agate Bay is a place similar to that just described. It lies a short distance west of the Hot Springs.

CRYSTAL BAY.— This beautiful cove forms the extreme north end of Lake Tahoe. It lies northeast of Hot Springs.

SHAKESPEARE ROCK.—In sailing round the lake from Tahoe City to Glenbrook several picturesque rocky points, studded with stately pines, will be seen, also Shakespeare Rock, which is a cliff towering high above the level of the lake. On the face of this cliff are seen ridges, fissures, and patches of color which at a distance resolve themselves into the likeness of the face of the immortal dramatist.

CAVE ROCK is passed before reaching Glenbrook. It is about 300 feet in height and seen from the deck of the steamer, towers upward like the castle of some "Blue Beard" giant of the Sierras. It has in its face a yawning cavern some 80 feet in depth. In this dark cave one might suppose the giant to live.

GLENBROOK is on the east side of the lake near a large cave. Here are several large saw-mills, owned by Yerington, Bliss & Co., which manufacture an immense quantity of all kinds of lumber. The mills are furnished with electrical lights. The mill company have here a narrow-gauge railroad nine miles in length, which carries their lumber and timber to the flumes at the top of the mountain (Eastern Summit), whence it is floated down to the valley near Carson City.

CASCADE MOUNTAIN, at the south end of the lake, is 9,500 feet in height. Near it are beautiful cascades, and from the top are to be seen a number of small lakes, and much wild and grand mountain scenery.

RUBICON SPRINGS, which lie just over the Western Summit of the Sierras, are easily reached by a good stage road from McKinneys'. Here, on the headwaters of the Rubicon River, is some of the most charming scenery to be found anywhere in the mountains. There are innumerable nooks, in which the disposition and proportions of water, foliage, and rugged granite rocks is such that all would seem to have been arranged for the special delectation of the artist and the lover of nature. The water of the springs at this place possesses wonderful curative powers. No invalid ever left them with a feeling of disappointment, however highly they might have been recommended to him.

Besides the places named there are scores of nooks and corners, cliffs, streams, fountains, canyons, and gorges that are not even honored with a name, which in almost any other part of the world would be lauded to the skies, and which would attract swarms of visitors from great distances. There is not a spot about the lake that would not astound the dweller in the prairies of the West were he placed before it.

Routes to Lake Tahoe.
THE ROUTE FROM TRUCKEE.

Persons in California, or tourists bound East, who wish to visit Tahoe will leave the Central Pacific at Truckee. The distance to the lake is but fourteen miles, over a good stage-road, which passes along up the Truckee River, amid grand and beautiful scenery. High, rocky, and picturesque mountains wall in the gorge through which winds the river and the road, and on all sides are groves of stately pines. In places where the walls recede from the stream are charming little nooks, valleys, and meadows. Indeed, at every turn in road and river new beauties are disclosed.

There are fresh surprises on every furlong of the road from Truckee to Tahoe City, which town is situated at the outlet of the lake which forms the

Truckee River. At Tahoe City will be found good hotels and accommodations of all kinds. Here, too, will be found in waiting a steamer to carry the visitor round the lake to Glenbrook, passing near the principal points of interest on the way, or to make the circuit of the lake. While to follow every projection and indentation of the shore-line would require a sail of 144 miles, a circuit of about 75 miles carries the visitor sufficiently near for a satisfactory view of the more charming and picturesque points.

Below are given the distances from Tahoe City to the principal points around the lake on the route usually taken by the steamers:—

Distances from Tahoe City.

MILES.

Tahoe City to McKinney's	7
Sugar-Pine Point	9
Emerald Bay	16
Tallac Mountain and Hotel	20
Rowlands	24
Glenbrook *via* Rowlands	34
Glenbrook, direct	14
Cornelian Bay	7½
Observatory	2½
Hot Springs	10
Round the lake	75

On his arrival at Glenbrook, the tourist that came *via* Truckee will find stages in waiting to carry him to Carson City, where he will take the Virginia and Truckee Railroad to the Central Pacific at Reno.

The Route from Reno.

The traveler from the East who wishes to view the wonders of Tahoe in passing across the continent, or to see the Comstock Silver Mines, will leave the Central Pacific at Reno, allowing his baggage to go on to his point of destination in California. The Virginia and Truckee will then take him to Carson City, a distance of thirty-one miles to the southward, passing through an interesting region all the way.

At Carson stages for Lake Tahoe will be found in waiting. The distance from Carson to Tahoe is fourteen miles. The road is fine, and the mountain scenery wild and beautiful. In passing up Clear Creek Canyon, the tourist will travel for a considerable distance alongside the big lumber flume of the Carson and Tahoe Lumber Company. This flume is in the shape of the letter V. It has a length of twenty-one miles. Through it runs a small stream of water, and a stick of timber, billet of wood, or piece of lumber dropped into the V-shaped trough at the summit at once darts away at race-horse speed, and very shortly thereafter is dumped at the wood and lumber yard at Carson. In one day may thus be sent down the flume 700 cords of wood, or 500,000 feet of mining timbers. Hank Monk, the famous stage-driver who for a long time drove over this piece of road, and who once "hurled" Horace Greeley from the summit of the Sierras down into Placerville, is now dead, and lies buried at Carson City.

On arriving at Glenbrook, the traveler will find ready a steamer which will take him round Lake Tahoe to Tahoe City, whence he will take a stage-coach fourteen miles down the Truckee River to the Central Pacific, at the town of Truckee.

The Town of Truckee.

Truckee is situated in a heavily-timbered basin, lying between the two ridges, or summits, of the Sierras. In this basin is contained an area of over 250 square miles of as fine pine forest as is to be found in the mountains. The town is the center of a great and flourishing lumbering industry, and immense quantities of ice are each winter harvested and stored in the immediate vicinity. In 1883 it was estimated that the forests of Truckee Basin contained 5,000,000,000 feet of lumber, and that 50,000,000 feet might be cut every year for 100 years. The town has an elevation of 5,866 feet, or over a mile above the level of the sea, yet for eight months of the year the climate is pleasant. Where the town now stands was formerly "Coburn's Station," on the old Dutch Flat wagon-road. The place was named Truckee, and began to build up in 1865, with the construction of the Central Pacific Railroad at that point. It is a brisk and thriving place, and, besides its lumber and ice industries, has a good trade with an extensive farming and grazing region. It is wonderful that so large a town exists as is now seen, in view of the fact that since 1868 it has seven times been swept by terrible fires, and by two or three of these it was, in different years, almost wiped out of existence.

Donner Lake.

This beautiful little sheet of water is but three miles from the town of Truckee, and is reached by a delightful drive over a smooth and level road. Donner Lake is about three miles long and from a mile to a mile and a half wide. It is about 200 feet in depth in the deepest place, and lies at an elevation of 5,938 feet above the level of the sea. It has for feeders several sparkling trout-brooks, and has an outlet called Donner Creek, which is an affluent of the Truckee River. The lake is full of trout of the same species as are found in Lake Tahoe, with minnows of several kinds, known as "chubs" and "white fish." It is a safe and beautiful lake on which to row or sail. As regards the matter of safety it may be set down as the "family lake" of the mountains—is as reliable and devoid of tantrums as the old "family mare." The lake is surrounded with grand old mountains. Lake Ridge, to the southward, rises to the height of 8,234 feet, and its lower part is covered with pine and other evergreen trees. To the west rise huge, bare granite mountains. The track of the Central Pacific Railroad runs along the side of the ridge to the southward, and presently disappears in a tunnel under the bald mountains in the west. Owing to the track being covered with snow-sheds, passengers get only occasional glimpses of the lake.

At the upper and lower ends of the lake are patches of meadow land, groves of pine and tamarack, and handsome clumps of willow and quaking asp. Donner is a favorite place of resort for camping parties from Nevada and California. There are grand views in all directions. Artists here find constant use for their sketching tools. A fine picture of the lake was painted by Bierstadt in 1872. He chose the month of August for his picture.

THE DONNER DISASTER.—At the foot of the lake is the scene of the sufferings of the Donner party. The spot is marked by a tall wooden cross. At this little mountain-begirt lake, in October, 1846, arrived a party of emigrants (mostly from Illinois), under the leadership of George Donner. There were with the train seventy-six men, women, and children. That winter the snow fell a month earlier than usual, and in a single night the party found themselves overwhelmed, caught in a *cul-de-sac*. It was impossible to attempt the mountains when the snow in the lower ground about the lake was so deep that the wagons could not be moved; besides, it snowed without ceasing. In one night, when their cattle were scattered about, snow fell to such a depth as to completly cover and hide them from sight. It was then decided to build cabins and winter on the spot. Being short of provisions, they at once killed all the cattle they could find, using the hides to roof the cabins. In December all provisions were exhausted, and parties were sent out one after another to reach California and there make known the condition of those left in the camp. Most of those thus sent out perished, but finally one or two persons reached Sutter's Fort, at Sacramento. The first relief parties failed, and it was not until February that a party reached the starving people of the camp. These, meantime, had been reduced to such extremity as to cook and eat the raw hides covering their cabins and the bones thrown away earlier in the season. Toward the last there was at least one instance of cannibalism. Of the seventy-six persons but forty survived, some perishing in the mountains (where the snow was thirty feet deep) in trying to get through to California, and others dying in the cabins. Those found in the cabins were mere skeletons. A thick volume would be required to give a full account of all the sufferings and trials of the ill-fated Donner party. It was a disaster that shocked all California for years, and which created a profound sensation of horror and pity throughout the whole United States. The history of what occurred at Donner Lake that winter has never been fully written, and never will be, as there were happenings that the survivors were never willing to talk about.

SURROUNDING POINTS OF INTEREST.—Donner Peak, to the west of the lake, a towering pile of granite, rises to a height of 8,154 feet above the level of the sea, and Clacial Point, in the same direction, is 7,708 feet in height. Fremont's Peak—sometimes called

Castle Peak, or Mount Stanford—towers in the northwest to the height of 9,237 feet above sea level. It is seen about four miles north of Summit Station. At this peak heads Pioneer Creek. From its granite pinnacle, on a clear day may be seen the Downieville Buttes, Marysville Buttes, the Coast Range, and many mountains and valleys in California; and looking eastward, Mount Davidson, the sinks of the Carson and Humboldt, are seen, with many other mountains and deserts. Near Summit are about a dozen small lakes, some of them charming both in themselves and in their surroundings of rocks and trees.

Independence Lake.

This beautiful lake is nineteen miles distant from Truckee, and is reached by stage or carriage. It is three miles long and three-quarters of a mile wide. The lake was named by Lola Montez (when a resident of Grass Valley, California) on the occasion of a visit to it on a picnic excursion, July 4, 1853. It is held up toward the heavens to a height of 7,000 feet by a circle of grand old peaks. It is very deep, and in places has never been fathomed. Owing to its great depth, the lake is supposed to occupy an extinct volcanic crater, whereas Donner Lake was formed by a moraine deposited across the valley by a glacier. The lake is alive with trout of a peculiar species, a good deal resembling brook trout, and for which they are often sold. The surrounding scenery is as wildly beautiful as the imagination can picture.

From the peak of Mount Lola, 4 miles north of the lake and 11,000 feet high, can be seen Mount Shasta, distant 180 miles to the northward; Mount Diablo, 140 miles distant; all Sacramento Valley, and scores of peaks of note in all directions. There is a hotel at the lake and good accommodations of all kinds. Bear, deer, and grouse are to be found in the chaparral, mountain glades, and pine forests. The lake has an outlet which is the head of one of the principal branches of the Little Truckee.

Webber Lake.

This lake lies twenty-five miles north of Truckee, and is reached by stage over a road bordered with charming scenery. The lake is circular in form and about a mile in diameter. It is 6,925 feet above sea-level. It is surrounded with mountains of graceful outline, nearly all of which are wooded to their tops. The deepest spot to be found measures only 80 feet. The lake is of glacial origin. It abounds in trout—a very game variety, introduced nearly thirty years ago. About the lake are numerous attractions. About a mile south from the lake, on a tributary creek, are falls over 100 feet in height; a mile north is a little gem of a lake, with an area of 50 acres, which is called the Lake of the Woods, and which is 7,500 feet (nearly a mile and a half) above the level of the sea; near at hand is Prospect Peak, from the top of which, in a clear day, mountain peaks distant 300 miles may be made out, while all about are other tall peaks and objects of interest. Small mountain game is plentiful near the lake. Bear may be found by those anxious to see them by taking a tramp in the chaparral thickets of the higher peaks. There is a good hotel at the lake, yet it is a great place of resort for campers. Where the greatest depth of water is only 80 feet, no one is afraid of drowning. The lake has an outlet, which is one of the affluents of the Little Truckee.

Pyramid Lake.

We have now to speak of a few Nevada lakes not mentioned in connection with the rivers of the State. The greatest of these, and the largest lake between the Sierra Nevada Range and the Rocky Mountains, except Great Salt Lake, Utah, is Pyramid Lake. It is fed by the Truckee, the course of which river has already been traced, and the head of which has been particularly described as the outlet of Lake Tahoe. Pyramid Lake lies in Washoe County, on the west line of Humboldt County. The lake is nearly 40 miles long by from 15 to 20 miles in width, and has an elevation of 4,000 feet above the level of the sea. It has no outlet. It is the most picturesque sheet of water in all the Great Basin region, owing to its numerous rocky islands. As it lies off the usual lines of travel and traffic it is seldom visited, yet it is well worthy of the attention of the tourist. Pyramid Lake lies about 25 miles north of Wadsworth, a brisk and thriving town on the Central Pacific Railroad. It is at Wadsworth that the traveler by rail from the East first reaches the Truckee River, and is where the traveler from California takes his leave of the stream. At Wadsworth the river turns abruptly to the north, which course it holds to the lake.

A vehicle for a trip to the lake can always be found at Wadsworth. The road lies down along the timbered banks of the river, and here and there will be seen the cabins of the Indians of the Pyramid Reservation. Most of the groves seen are of cottonwood and willow trees. The Truckee River has two mouths, one of which empties into Pyramid Lake and the other into Winnemucca Lake. The branch which feeds Pyramid Lake is only about one mile in length, whereas the more meandering branch, which is the feeder of Winnemucca Lake, has a length of six miles.

Pyramid Lake contains several islands. Some of these, near the middle of the lake, are pyramidal in shape, and gray in color. They rise to a height of several hundred feet above the surface of the water, and it is from these natural pyramids that the lake takes its name. Far away toward the north end of the lake is seen a tall, slender pyramid that is perfectly white. Some of the isolated rocks seen are egg-shaped, and 300 to 400 feet high. Fremont's Pyramid is the name borne by one of the taller of the pyramidal rocks near the head of the lake. One of the largest islands contains large flocks of goats, the progeny of a few pairs of the animals turned loose there many years ago. The island has an area of about five square miles, and is well covered with vegetation, being less precipitous and rocky than the others. The only picturesque addition needed to this island is a "Crusoe" and his hut.

One small, rocky island is wholly given up to rattlesnakes. It is the home of thousands of the venomous reptiles. They have their dens in the rocks, and live upon the eggs and young of water-fowl, and such small fish as are cast ashore.

Pyramid Lake is of immense depth. No one knows its depth in the deepest part. At the last attempt to sound it, 600 fathoms (3,600 feet) of line were run out without finding bottom. Where it enters the lake the water of the Truckee River is as pure and sweet as where it leaves Lake Tahoe, yet the water of Pyramid Lake is slightly brackish. However, myriads of trout are found in Pyramid Lake. The Piute Indians of the Reservation every year catch and sell thousands of tons of trout, deriving a snug sum from this source. The lake never freezes, and is generally very rough. The Indian fishermen, however, navigate its waters at all times quite fearlessly, even when seated astride of a bundle of tules.

Winnemucca Lake.

This lake lies to the east of, and parallel with, Pyramid Lake, from which it is separated by only a single ridge of gray rock and sand. It lies principally in Humboldt County, though a part reaches south into Churchill County. The lake is now about sixty miles long, with an average width of twelve miles. Of late years it has been rapidly increasing in size, as more water has been flowing through its feeder than formerly. It has on the east side a high rocky ridge, like that which separates it from Pyramid, therefore it lies in a trough between two ranges of hills. Though so near to each other, the surface of the water in Winnemucca Lake is forty feet lower than that in Pyramid. The Piutes remember a time when all was one lake. Were the waters of these twin lakes now united they would make a lake quite as large as the great Salt Lake of Utah. The inlet to Winnemucca Lake contains several old rafts of drift-wood, which prevent a free flow of water through it. Some years ago a freshet lifted these rafts from the bed of the stream, and the water found a channel beneath them. Since that occurred Winnemucca Lake has been steadily increasing in size. There are many Indian traditions connected with these lakes, one of which is in regard to immense animals that once herded in the neighborhood. This seems to be a tradition of the elephant or mastodon. All this region was once covered by an inland sea of fresh water, over 200 miles in length, and 80 or 90 miles in width.

Washoe Lake.

Washoe Lake is situated in Washoe Valley, and is seen in going by rail from Reno to Carson. The lake proper is about four miles long, and from a mile to a mile and a half wide. On the west and north extend large tule marshes, which at times contain a considerable depth of water. The lake is fed by small streams from the Sierras, and it has an outlet into Steamboat Creek. The lake is filled with perch and catfish, planted a few years ago; also contains swarms of native fish of the "chub" species. It is a favorite resort for anglers from Carson and the towns of the Comstock. At certain seasons the lake is visited by great numbers of ducks, geese, and other water-fowl. It is shallow, and, having a muddy bottom, it is not a suitable sheet of water for either brook or lake trout. Carp, however, would flourish in its muddy depths and tule shallows.

Thermal and Medicinal Springs.

The hot springs of Nevada are numbered by thousands and tens of thousands, and scores of them in all parts of the State possess more or less medicinal value. Hot springs are found from the Oregon and Idaho lines southward to the Colorado River, and from the eastern base of the Sierras across the whole breadth of the State. No one has ever attempted to number the many warm and hot springs, and they are literally innumerable. Springs which would attract great attention in the Atlantic States, and which would be worth fortunes, here pass unknown, unnamed, "unhonored and unsung." All the hot springs possess curative properties in the case of rheumatic and various skin diseases. Not one in a thousand of the springs on this side of the Sierras has been analyzed, for which reason the waters of only a few are used internally.

Steamboat Springs.

The most noted hot springs in the western part of Nevada are those known as the Steamboat Springs. They were so named by the first white men who visited them, on account of the puffing sound some of them then emitted, and because of the tall columns of steam they sent up. These springs are in Steamboat Valley, ten miles south of Reno. The Virginia and Truckee Railroad passes close alongside the springs. They are situated at the eastern base of a low range of basaltic hills, and occupy the top of a flat ridge that is over a mile in length and has a north and south course. This ridge is about half a mile in width and is composed of a whitish silicious material evidently deposited by the waters of the many springs.

The temperature of the principal springs is 204 degrees, which is as hot as water can be made at that altitude (5,000 feet above the level of the sea). Some of the springs rise through circular openings from a foot to three feet in diameter and are surrounded by conical mounds of silicious matters deposited by the waters, whereas others flow from fissures, which are evidently rents formed by earthquakes. Out of some of these fissures rush great volumes of hot gases that have a strong odor of sulphur. These fissures are perfectly dry, and the jets of hot air are invisible. From other dry crevices issue great clouds of very hot steam. Steam rises in great volumes from all the boiling springs, and of mornings when the air is cool and calm from 60 to 80 tall pillars of steam may be counted, rising to a height of 100 feet or more above the low, bare ridge. The air everywhere about the springs is strongly charged with sulphurous vapors in gases. The crevices have the same course as the great quartz veins of the country, *i. e.*, northeast and southwest. Here is no doubt a huge metallic vein in process of formation; indeed, various minerals are deposited by the gases, notably cinnabar. Some of the fissures may be traced from 1,000 to 3,000 feet, and have a width of from 16 inches to 3 feet. In places where nothing is seen to issue from these fissures at the surface, indications of tremendous subterranean activity are distinctily audible. Far down in under-ground regions are heard thunderous surgings and lashings as of huge volumes of water dashed to and fro in vast hollow, resounding caverns. In other places are heard fearful (dry) thumpings and poundings, as though at some flaming forge below a band of sweating Cyclops were at work at hammering out thunder-bolts for old Jove.

Small springs in places send jets of hot water into

the air to the height of two or three feet, with a hissing and sputtering sound, but for some years past none of them have thrown water to any great distance above the surface. In 1860, and for a few years thereafter, two or three of the springs rivaled the geysers of Yellowstone Park, sending columns of water a yard in diameter to a height of sixty or eighty feet once in from six to eight hours. Some springs sent columns of water from three to six inches in diameter to a still greater height. Even now the water is seen to rise and fall in some of the fissures in a threatening manner. At the springs is a fine and commodious hotel, bathing-houses for vapor baths, and every desirable accommodation. The springs are very beneficial to persons afflicted with rheumatic complaints, and are also useful in some cases of cutaneous diseases.

Shaw's Springs.

These springs are situated about a mile west of Carson City. They are also much frequented by persons afflicted with rheumatism and kindred complaints, though more well than sick persons use the baths, as connected with them is a large swimming pool, 60 by 24 feet and from $4\frac{1}{2}$ to $5\frac{1}{2}$ feet deep. One of these springs is what is called a "chicken-soup" spring. By adding pepper and salt to the water it acquires the taste of thin chicken soup.

State Prison Warm Springs.

About a mile east of Carson City, at the Nevada State prison, is a warm spring of great volume.

Here Col. Abe Curry, who owned the property before it was acquired by the State, constructed the first swimming bath to be found on the Pacific Coast. It is 160 feet long by 38 feet wide, and is walled up with stone, and over it is erected a building, also of stone, of which there is a fine quarry on the spot. The water in the pool is from three to five feet deep, and is of about blood heat. This bath is not now open to the "world at large," but is kept for a little world that is "not at large."

Walley's Springs.

There are in hundreds of places along the eastern base of the Sierras groups of hot springs of more or less celebrity, but none of which are more highly esteemed for their curative properties, or as a more popular place of resort for the afflicted, than Walley's Springs, a mile and a half south of Genoa. Persons who are troubled with rheumatism, or are afflicted with scrofula and like disorders, are much benefited by the baths at these springs. Here are also excellent mud baths, the hot, mineral-impregnated mud being found very efficacious in many cases of chronic rheumatic complaints. In the vicinity are many objects of interest, and near at hand may be found good hunting and fishing. There is a fine hotel, and the best of accommodations of every kind for both sound and sick, at the springs. The springs are fourteen and a half miles south of Carson and may be reached either by stage or private conveyance. The road lies through Carson Valley, and is fine and smooth.

Other Springs.

Near Elko are several hot springs, with fine springs of cold water in their immediate vicinity. Here, too, is a "chicken-soup" spring. The springs are situated to the northwest of the town, and a bathing-house has been erected for the accommodation of the rheumatic public.

At Golconda are some very large hot springs, near which are others of ordinary temperature. Some of the hot springs are occasionally utilized for scalding hogs. In the cool pools connected with the flow from the hot springs, carp and some other kinds of fish have been planted. It is said that the carp grown in the ponds often venture upon darting through places where water almost boiling hot is bubbling up. These springs are near the Central Pacific Railroad station. Also half a mile south of the track of the Central Pacific road there are, at Hot Springs Station, near the sink of the Humboldt, several springs that send up columns of steam.

There are only a few of the hot springs that are situated near main lines of travel. In Thousand Spring Valley, on the Upper Humboldt, there are literally thousands of springs, some of which send out whole brooks of water. The majority of these, however, are cold. In Churchill County, north of the Sand Springs salt marsh, are hot springs which are 50, 80, and even 100 feet in diameter. They are on the edge of a desert at the foot of a range of rocky hills burnt to a brick-red by volcanic fires. Here, too, are seen thick veins of pure native sulphur. There are hot springs and scalding pools and brooks in every county in the State. In Nye County there are many hot springs in Hot Creek Valley, in Big Smoky Valley, and Lone Valley. There is also in this county the Cabezon Valley Hot Spring, which is medicinal. On the Rio Virgin, in Lincoln County, is one of the finest purgative springs on the Pacific Coast. With other ingredients amounting to 311 grains of solid matter to the gallon, it contains 67 grains of sulphate of soda, 54 grains of sulphate of magnesia, and 3 grains of sulphate of potassa.

Railroads in Nevada.

Although Nevada would appear at a first glance a difficult region in which to construct railroads, the fact is that it is quite the contrary. Between the parallel ranges of mountains running north and south, there are long level valleys, tracts of desert land, requiring very little grading. These valleys and deserts are linked together and connected by plains from the northern to the southern boundary of the State. As these valleys and deserts once formed the beds and connecting channels of chains of lakes now extinct, it is evident that in following their course a line of railroad might be very cheaply constructed. In many places for miles on miles there would be little to do but put down the ties and rails. In many places, too, there are remarkable passages leading east and west from valley to valley, called "gates." There are clean level east and west cuts through ranges of mountains running north and south. The only difficulty to be encountered in railroad building in Nevada is in running roads to special points (as to mines) high above the general level of the country, as in the case of the Virginia to Truckee when it leaves the valley region to climb the Mount Davidson Range to the Comstock Lode. The whole plateau through which was upheaved the north and south ranges of mountains has a mean elevation of 5,000 feet above the level of the sea in all central Nevada; to the southward it gradually slopes downward, until at the south line of the State, on the Colorado River, the altitude above sea-level is only 800 feet.

The Central Pacific.

The largest stretch of railroad in Nevada is the Central Pacific. Its length within the boundaries of the State, from where it enters, near Verdi, to where it passes out, near Tecoma, is a little over 450 miles. Though this is an east and west road (the course across the interior parallel mountain ranges), yet no great difficulties were encountered in crossing the State. The road enters Nevada from California along the course of the Truckee River, which stream it follows as far east as Wadsworth. Leaving Wadsworth the road traverses a level, sandy plain till the Humboldt River is reached. The road then follows the course of the Humboldt to Cedar Pass, not far from the Utah line.

The Virginia and Truckee.

Having already given a description of this road, it will not be necessary in this place to do more than to mention the distance from point to point between Reno and Virginia City. Soon after leaving Reno the dumps of the flumes that bring wood and lumber down from the pine forests of the Sierras will be seen to the right of the road. The first of these is four miles from Reno; three miles farther on, near Huffaker's Station, is another, and at Brown's is a third. Others will be seen about Washoe Valley and Franktown. They are from ten to twenty miles in length, and of the same V-shape as that at Carson City. Steamboat Springs Station is eleven miles from Reno; Washoe, sixteen miles; Franktown, twenty-one miles; Carson City, thirty-one miles; Carson to Empire, three miles; Mexican Mill, three and one-fourth; Morgan Mill, four; Brunswick, five; Merrimac, five and one-half; Vivian, six; Santiago Mill, seven miles; Mound House, ten; Silver Switch, twelve and three-fourths; Scales, sixteen and one-half; Baltic Switch, seventeen and one-half; Crown Point, eighteen; Gold Hill, nineteen; Virginia City, twenty-one miles from Carson and fifty-two from Reno.

Carson and Colorado.

At Mound House, ten miles from Carson City, the Carson and Colorado Narrow Gauge Railroad connects with the Virginia and Truckee. This road runs southeasterly through Lyon and Esmeralda Counties, in Nevada, then, turning more south, passes through a corner of Mono County, California, and enters Inyo County in the same State. It has a total length of 293 miles, and its present southern terminus is at Keeler, at the south end of Owen's Lake, Inyo County. The road passes through regions of very diverse products and industries. Agricultural and grazing sections alternate with those in which the ruling pursuit is mining for the precious metals, and these with others where are immense salt, soda, and borax marshes.

Six miles from Mound House is Dayton, on the Carson River. It is a milling town with agricultural surroundings. The road runs eastward near the course of the Carson River through a fine agricultural and grazing country, then turns southward through Churchill Canyon to the town of Wabuska, thirty-eight miles.

WABUSKA is a thriving little place at the edge of Mason Valley, one of the finest agricultural and grazing regions in the State, the Walker River affording excellent facilities for irrigation. After leaving Wabuska, Walker Lake is soon reached. The road passes along the eastern shore of the lake nearly its whole length, affording many fine and picturesque views. It is a beautiful sheet of water, but lacks trees and vegetation, hardly a green thing being seen on its shores, except at the upper end, at and about the mouth of the Walker River.

Hawthorne, 100 miles from Mound House, is situated about 3½ miles beyond the foot of the lake. Although only a little more than eight years old, the town is beginning to present a comfortable appearance. It stands on a plain the soil of which at the time the town was laid out seemed to be nothing better than pure sand, yet on such a foundation has been conjured an oasis of shady groves, blooming grounds, and productive gardens. The town has a population of about 600. There are many small veins of gold and silver-bearing quartz in the surrounding mountains that are rich and easily worked. Here stages leave for Aurora, 26, and Bodie, 37 miles to the southward. Much freight is taken by team from Hawthorne to the two mining towns named. The Walker Lake *Bulletin*, a good local paper, is published weekly in the town.

Luning, 125 miles from Mound House, is in the midst of a mining region the veins of which have about the same characteristics as those about Hawthorne. Stages and teams leave the town for Downieville, Grantsville, and Belmont.

Belleville, 150 miles from Mound House, is a thriving mining and milling town.

Candelaria, 158 miles from Mound House, is a brisk mining town of about 600 inhabitants. It contains several mines of note, and has yielded great quantities of bullion. The Mt. Diablo Mine is at the present time the leading bullion producer. The town has several mills, some good buildings, and a good system of water works. Stages leave the town for Columbus, Silver Peak, Montezuma, Alida Valley, and Gold Mountain.

Leaving Candelaria, the road soon passes into California, striking down into Independence Valley near the White Mountains, the highest peak of which stands 12,000 feet above the level of the sea. The line runs through a rich agricultural and grazing region, with high mountain ranges on either hand, in which are found many veins rich in the precious metals.

BENTON, in Mono County, California, is 193 miles from Mound House. It is situated in a rich section of Independence Valley and is a fine fruit-growing region. In the neighborhood of the town, which contains about 200 inhabitants, are many good farms, orchards, and vineyards.

BISHOP CREEK is a flourishing agricultural settlement, 224 miles from Mound House. It is in Inyo County. The lands and surroundings are much the same as those of Benton. The hamlet constituting the trading-post at the railroad, and the farms in the neighborhood, have a population of about 250.

INDEPENDENCE, 267 miles from Mound House, with the farms in its immediate neighborhood, has a population of about 400. The town stands in the midst of a fine farming, grazing, and fruit-growing region. Bordering the valley are mountains in which are many good mines of the precious metals, though these have been but little worked and many have not been opened at all, the settlers in the valleys who discovered them being devoted to agricultural pursuits. Here is published weekly the *Inyo Independent*, an excellent local paper.

KEELER, the present terminus of the Carson and Colorado Railroad, is 293 miles from Mound House. The town is situated on the east side of Owens Lake and near its south end. It is a new place and contains only about 200 inhabitants. Stages leave the town for Cerro Gordo, Darwin, and Panamint. Owens Lake, which is the "sink" of Owens River, has an area of about 110 square miles. Its waters are heavily charged with salt and alkaline minerals. One United States standard gallon (8⅓ pounds, or 231 cubic inches) of the lake water contains 4,422.25 grains of solid matter, sodium carbonate and sodium chloride predominating and aggregating 2,561.83 grains.

The water of the lake contains only a trace of borax. It is evaporated on a large scale near Keeler, for the valuable alkaline minerals it holds in solution. The water of Owens Lake contains a much greater quantity of mineral matter than that of the Dead Sea. In Dead Sea water there is only 1,680 grains of solid matter to the United States gallon. Dead Sea water is evidently less salt than that of many of the lakes of the Great Basin region, as fish are found in it at and near the mouths of tributary streams, and in places along its shores shell-fish are to be seen. Mono Lake, about 100 miles north of Owens Lake, in Mono County, has an area of 85 square miles. Its water is almost precicely similar in every respect to that of Owens Lake.

Owens River, over 100 miles in length, flows through the valley nearly its whole course, and, with its many tributary creeks, affords water sufficient to irrigate a great area of land. The whole region is rapidly being taken by settlers. The soil is exceedingly fertile and the climate very fine. To the west of the chain of valleys the snow-clad Sierras tower to a vast height. Above all surrounding peaks Mount Whitney rises to a height of 15,000 feet. The Carson and Colorado road will eventually be extended southward to a connection with the railroad system of Southern California.

Eureka and Palisade.

This railroad is ninety miles in length. It is a narrow gauge and connects Eureka with the Central Pacific at Palisade. It was constructed to transport machinery and supplies to the mines and town of Eureka, and to carry out the products of the smelting furnaces. Palisade contains about 250 inhabitants.

EUREKA is a town of smelting furnaces. It is situated in the midst of a region in which very rich smelting ores are mined. The mines at Eureka were discovered in 1864, but not much was done with them until two years later, and in 1869 the place began to boom and the yield of the mines soon became from one to three millions of dollars annually. Like other mining towns, Eureka has its ebbs and flows of fortune. For a year or two it was in "barrasca," but since the beginning of 1888 it has been again getting into "bonanza." It is the county seat of Eureka County, and has a population of about 2,500. In 1880 it had a population of 4,207, but in 1886-87 it lost inhabitants. Now it is once more gaining. It is the point from which many interior mining towns and camps receive their supplies. There are many fine and substantial public and private buildings in the town, and a good system of water works. In the *Sentinel*, published weekly, the place has a good local paper. Eureka is the Pittsburg of Nevada. In all directions its furnace chimneys vomit volumes of black, sulphurous smoke—when Government officials do not "pester" the people on account of their cutting scrub timber.

Nevada Central.

This road is a narrow gauge, 93 miles in length, and connects Austin with the Central Pacific at Battle Mountain. From Battle Mountain the road runs nearly south up the valley of the Reese River. There are many good farms in Reese River Valley, and good grazing ranges on the higher ground.

BATTLE MOUNTAIN is a town of about 500 inhabitants, situated very pleasantly, and cheaply supplied with water by means of artesian wells of trifling depth. Its business is derived from the surrounding farming and grazing regions, from the Central Pacific Railroad, and from the several mining sections with which it has communication. It contains many good public and private buildings, and handsome cottages are numerous. The *Central Nevadan*, a sprightly weekly paper, is published in the town.

AUSTIN is the oldest town in Eastern Nevada, and the mother of mining in that part of the State. It is the county seat of Lander County. Austin was laid out in February, 1863. It is situated nearly upon the summit of the Toyabee Range of mountains, about six miles from Reese River, and is nearly in the geographical center of the State. It contains many good, substantial public and private buildings of brick and stone. Before the completion of the Central Pacific the overland stages passed through the town, when it had about 5,000 inhabitants, as it was also then the center of a rich mining region. The mines at and about Austin have produced many millions in gold and silver bullion. Like all other mining towns, Austin has had her periods of elevation and depression—her "streaks of fat and streaks of lean"—and this year (1889) seems to be getting out of a lean streak into a streak that shows a considerable amount of "fatty" matter. August 18, 1874, the town was nearly ruined by a cloud-burst which tore up the roadway and sidewalks of the main street, flooded buildings, and filled them with mud and sand to the depth of several feet. The damage done was estimated at $100,000. As the people had warning of what was coming, no lives were lost. In this the Austinites were more fortunate than were the people of Eureka in the month of July, in the same year, as there a cloud-burst not only did immense damage to the town, but also drowned fifteen persons. An excellent daily paper, the *Reese River Reveille*, is published at Austin.

Nevada and California.

This narrow-gauge railroad starts at Reno and runs northward into Lassen County, California. It has now attained a length of about eighty miles, and is still in process of construction. It is penetrating a region of country containing vast forests of pine timber, good mines, and many fine mountain valleys. Eventually it will be run northward into the interior of Oregon. It will presently bring to Reno great quantities of lumber and timber to be shipped eastward into the timberless regions of the Great Basin country.

Proposed Railroads.

A section of railroad of narrow gauge has been constructed through the Beckworth Pass westward. It connects with the Nevada and California road at Moran, and is called the Sierra Valley and Mohawk Railroad. After rails had been laid through the pass and a short distance down the western slope of the

Sierras, work was discontinued. It is supposed that the section of road was laid in the interest of some one of the great Eastern roads now heading toward the Pacific Ocean in order to hold the pass. The Beckworth Pass is nearly 2,000 feet lower than that through which the Central Pacific Railroad is laid.

THE SALT LAKE AND LOS ANGELES is a proposed railroad on which surveying parties have been engaged for nearly a year. It is intended to start at Milford, on the Utah Central, pass through Lincoln County, Nevada, and connect with the railroad system of Southern California at Barstow. This road would tap a rich mining and a fine agricultural and grazing region in Southern Nevada. It would give life to an immense region of country that has long lain as dead.

Another proposed road is an extension of the Nevada Central from Battle Mountain northward into Idaho.

Nevada a Land of Great Possibilities.

Notwithstanding its sterile and forbidding appearance, Nevada is capable of supporting an immense population. The soil, which to the eyes of strangers appears so poor and barren, is one of the strongest and richest in America. It is formed of decomposed lava and various kinds of volcanic rocks, and contains large quantities of all the various mineral constituents necessary to a strong and healthy growth of every kind of farm produce known to the temperate zone. All that is required to produce a rank growth of vegetation of every kind is a supply of water; all other life-giving agents are contained in the soil. On the mountain slopes and the bench-lands, which look so arid and worthless, the soil is even stronger and more kindly than in the valleys. With water all the mountain-sides may be made veritable hanging gardens. Until within the past year agriculture (as regards irrigation) has been left to take care of itself. It has been left to individuals, each working after a plan of his own. There has been no established system of irrigation, and, save in one or two instances, no attempt at storing water in order to maintain a large and regular supply. The water used is taken as it flows from the mountains, as the snow banks deposited in winter melt away in the early spring and first summer months. Then, in average seasons, there are for a month or two floods of water pouring down all the rivers, creeks, and canyons. This great rush of water passes down into the interior lakes and "sinks" without being utilized for any purpose, and is lost. Were this water caught up in storage reservoirs ten times the area of land at present irrigated could be brought under cultivation.

At last a movement has been made toward the systematic reclamation of the arid lands of Nevada, and the proper storage and utilization of all the available water in the State. In November, 1888, a corps of U. S. Engineers began a hydrographic survey on the headwaters of the Truckee, Carson and Walker Rivers. This survey—interrupted by the cold weather of winter—will be completed this year. Already a survey of 800 square miles has been completed. Major Powell says Lake Tahoe constitutes an immense natural storage reservoir of almost incalculable value. He estimates that in it may be stored sufficient water (with a four-foot dam) to irrigate 500,000 acres of land. If this be true, then Donner Lake may be made to contain water sufficient to irrigate from 150,000 to 200,000 acres. On the headwaters of the Carson and Walker Rivers are many lakes and basins of extinct lakes that may be turned into vast storage reservoirs at small cost.

Among the mountain ranges of the interior of the State many reservoirs may be profitably constructed. Also in the interior valleys and basins artesian wells will be of great value. Already there are in the State 110 flowing wells. Though the flow from some of these is strong it is trifling to what might be obtained at greater depth, the present wells being only from 100 to 300 feet deep. Artesian water has been found to exist everywhere in the valleys lying between the mountain ranges of the interior.

Last winter the State government for the first time took hold of the irrigation question and made a move toward the establishment of a system of reservoirs and other works, appropriating $100,000 therefor.

To the southward of the line of the Central Pacific

158   THE STATE OF NEVADA.

l⸺s a region of country large enough to make half a dozen New England States, that is almost unoccupied. There tens of thousands of families might find homes. Lack of transportation facilities at present prevents settlers from going into that portion of the State, but the building of the Salt Lake and Los Angeles, or any other of the proposed railroads, would cause a rush to its semi-tropical valleys.

A beginning having been made, the time is not distant when Nevada will no longer be branded as a land whose soil is only capable of supporting the jack-rabbit, the lizard, and the horned-toad.

Printed in the United States
144755LV00006B/133/A